SCHOOL-AGE PARENTS

Other Books by Jeanne Lindsay:

Teens Parenting: The Challenge of Babies and Toddlers
Do I Have a Daddy? A Story About a Single-Parent Child
Teenage Marriage: Coping with Reality
Teens Look at Marriage: Rainbows, Roles and Reality
Parents, Pregnant Teens and the Adoption Option
Pregnant Too Soon: Adoption Is an Option
Open Adoption: A Caring Option

By Jeanne Lindsay and Sharon Rodine:
Teen Pregnancy Challenge, Book One:
Strategies for Change
Teen Pregnancy Challenge, Book Two:
Programs for Kids

By Jeanne Lindsay and Catherine Monserrat:
Adoption Awareness: Help for Teachers,
Counselors, Nurses and Caring Others

SCHOOL-AGE PARENTS
The Challenge
of
Three-Generation Living

Jeanne Warren Lindsay, M.A., C.H.E.

Morning Glory Press

Buena Park, California

Copyright © 1990 by Jeanne Warren Lindsay

All Rights Reserved

Library of Congress Cataloging-in-Publication Data

Lindsay, Jeanne Warren
    School-age parents : the challenge of three-generation living /
Jeanne Warren Lindsay.
      224 p. cm.
      Includes bibliographical references (p. 213-220) and index.
      ISBN 0-930934-37-7 (cloth) : $17.95. -- ISBN 0-930934-36-9
(pbk.) $10.95
      1. Teenage parents--United States. 2. Intergenerational
relations--United States.   I. Title
HQ759.64.L56   1990
306.87--dc20   90-6039
                                             CIP

MORNING GLORY PRESS, INC.
6595 San Haroldo Way   Buena Park, CA 90620
(714) 828-1998
Printed and bound in the United States of America

Contents

To the teenage parents
and their families
who share their lives
so generously on these pages

Preface

Before I started working with pregnant teenagers, I met the mother of one. I was startled to hear this obviously caring mother say, "At first we were horrified at her pregnancy, but then we said to ourselves, 'Why, this is a lot better than drinking or drugs.'"

But "drinking and drugs" can be for a short term, I thought. A baby is forever. I was thinking of the tremendous life style changes brought about by premature pregnancy, the lost dreams, the aborted college plans, the likelihood of a lifetime of poverty for the young woman who bears a child before she finishes high school.

Later, when I was hired to start a school program for pregnant and parenting teens, I remembered that woman's comment. It began to make sense as I met young women who were trying to break out of that trap which so often follows too-early parenting. Many of our students had good family support, and they were going to be all right.

At the same time, I began to hear more and more about the difficulties of three-generation living. These are normal teenagers with the not so normal problem of being someone's mother while still playing the role of being someone's child as well. The resulting dichotomy is bound to cause problems.

But some families are coping. Not perfectly, but quite well. Grandparents occasionally tell me how well their daughter is parenting their grandchild. Daughters tell me their parents expect them to take responsibility for their children but encourage them to go out occasionally while they (the grandparents) care for the baby.

I hear about parents who don't push marriage, but neither do they attempt to push the young father out of the picture. I see some of these young mothers—and fathers—struggling to complete their high school education and obtain job skills, and succeeding. Sometimes they will comment that their parents' help is important. More often, I don't hear that point of view until one, two, or several years later.

As I talk with teenage parents and their parents, a pattern begins to emerge. It's not a pattern that solves all the problems, but it does provide guidelines for families facing the shock of a daughter's too-early pregnancy (or the pregnancy of a son's partner) and the dilemma of teenage parenthood within the family.

In the following chapters, these young people and their parents share the pain *and the promise* of early parenting. They talk about the early weeks and months after the pregnancy is diagnosed, of the labor and delivery, and the return home with the baby. They describe the compromises so necessary in any multi-person household, but even more crucial, in a household made up of a teenager, her/his baby, and the teenager's parents. Their hope and mine is that their insight and experience will help others.

Jeanne Warren Lindsay
April, 1990

Foreword

Adolescent pregnancy—a phrase to strike terror in a parent's heart. As Jeanne Lindsay's book points out, it will be a crisis faced by approximately a half-million families in our country each year. The teenagers themselves, the unborn child, and the prospective grandparents and greatgrandparents are all impacted. All see their lives changed, temporarily or permanently. Life plans are altered, sometimes dramatically. A teenager may not go to college. A grandmother may find herself taking care of a newborn baby, a job she most likely had not envisioned for herself, and one for which she may have strongly mixed feelings. So where do these families turn for help?

The author, Jeanne Lindsay, has given us a resource for addressing these problems that owes its usefulness to a unique format. She eases into all the myriad problems created by a teenage unplanned pregnancy through the words and experiences of those individuals who have been involved.

Extensive interviews were conducted with the members of immediate as well as extended families, and the volunteers and professionals who work with this client population. Jeanne lets thoughts and feelings, rather than theories and statistics, document the scope of the problem for families and communities.

Her interviewees reveal in their own words their anguish, their pain, their confusion. They also candidly record their actions—the mistakes, the triumphs. The professionals add lessons learned from their efforts to help. Together their viewpoints give the reader an upfront and personal picture of the emotions of those faced with this crisis, indicate the practical problems of all of the individuals involved, and offer many clues as to the key elements in positive solutions for this real-life dilemma.

This personal, conversational approach to her book gives Jeanne an excellent vehicle with which to transmit a warm, comfortable tone to her message that pulls the reader along effortlessly. This is not a dry book. It's filled with as much emotion and drama as a good novel. You will end up caring about the characters and, at the same time, become much more knowledgeable about the scope and nature of the problem. Chances are you will be surprised how many members of a family this problem impacts, and how profoundly it changes their lives.

For us, one of the most important messages in the book touches on a belief we have long felt about this particular crisis and about crises in general. Jeanne points out, through her interviewees, that a teenage pregnancy crisis, while certainly a major, major obstacle for the adolescents and their families, also has an upside. For some, it provides a focal point for life planning. Many times we have seen girls gain confidence out of wrestling with the many crucial and gut-wrenching decisions put in front of them, and then be able to transfer that into better coping responses in other areas of their lives such as education, work, and relationships.

Theoreticians have felt that positive resolution of a crisis can set the stage for better future adaptation to life's inevitable crises. We feel that we've seen it happen in our work with teenagers and their families, and that element of hope is present in the experiences of those whose stories Jeanne Lindsay has so skillfully made available to us.

Georg Simmel, a German sociologist, wrote about the seemingly incongruent fact that conflict often seems to pull people together in their efforts to battle a common foe. Certainly we saw that happen in the United States during the Second World War. We gave up our pots and pans and not a few pairs of silk hose, and scrimped to buy War Bonds. There was privation, discomfort, and fear, but there was also an equal place for ingenuity, courage, and a reward for working together.

This upside of the teenage pregnancy crisis is represented by the teen and the family that end up a closer unit as a result of the problems they've solved together. It's evidenced by teenagers who finish high school as part of a clearer idea of who they are and what they want. The problems solved may have given them a recipe for the problems ahead and the confidence to tackle them. My hat is off to Jeanne for reminding us that this crisis is not all tragedy.

But this crisis is a tough one, and Lindsay covers its issues thoroughly. Only someone who has intimate knowledge of teenage pregnancy would think to include a section about the effect on a new grandmother of having not only to pick up her daughter's adolescent clutter, but now mislaid baby items as well.

Although the author weaves a thread of optimism through her interviews, along the way she acquaints us with the sobering reality of the experience. She also gives many hints as to how those burdens can be lightened, usually again with help from the experiences and words of the people themselves.

The reader can learn how families have found solutions to the questions of who pays the bills, cleans up the mess, and disciplines the child. These suggestions can give hope to anyone facing this problem, for they come from practical experience rather than an ivory tower. They are answers that have been developed and implemented by people just like you and me.

David Peterson, Ed.D., School Psychologist, Orange County,
     Florida
Judy Peterson, Director, BETA, Orlando, Florida

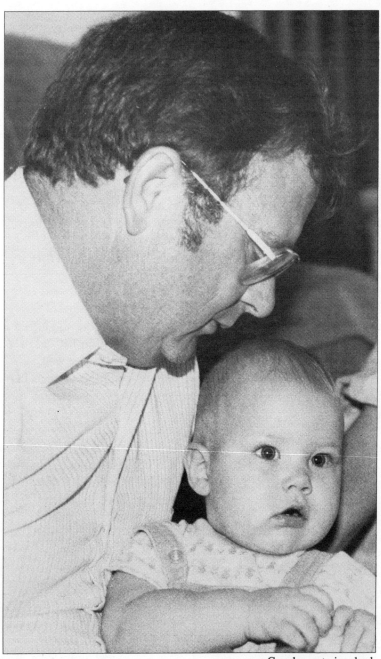

Grandpa gets involved.

Acknowledgments

The families who share their lives so generously on these pages are truly co-authors, and I appreciate them all. They were promised anonymity through the use of pseudonyms, but most of them gave me permission to list their real names here. They include Karen and Mike Overly, Janice Stout, and Lynn Jennings; Marie, Gary, and Lisa Shaw; Carolyn, Andy, and Suzanne Stefaniw; Marilyn and Leroy Andringa and Deanne Grachen; Joanne and Kim Taylor; Laura and Valerie Johnston; Becky, Alton, and Jeanette Brown; Dea Souza and Catherine Martinek; Linda and Michelle Harker; Linda, Bob, and Shelly Burke; Bill and Vicki Embree and Shanna Rurup; Marie, Vic, and Lynn Gilbert; Gwen, Pat, and Karen Nicks; Marilyn, Michael, and Debbie LaSalle; Alice and Jodie Spinneweber; Liane and Sheri Graessle; Pat Fleming and Carla Davenport; Marcie and Jim Mannan, Sue and Jason Samargis; Valerie Villarreal; Linda and Jennifer Van Duzer; Marge Eliason; Ron, Nicole, and Lissette Barger; Mary Lou and Dennis Jones, Julie and Joul Farah; Willi and Kay Klumper and Ardell Hucko; Joy and Jack Herritt; Kay, John, and Dana Morgan; Linda Gardner and Kimberly Hendrix.

Interviewing each person was an inspiring and exciting task. Writing a book in this fashion means I get to have my dessert first—my favorite part is listening as people share their lives in order that their experiences may help someone else.

I also deeply appreciate the help I received from professionals. Eugenie Wheeler shared her expertise both as a therapist and a writer. Her contributions in chapter twelve and her Afterword add a great deal to *School-Age Parents*. Judy and David Peterson contributed the delightful Foreword, and Judy also shared her counseling philosophy.

Talking with professionals, including Sally McCullough, Jean Brunelli, Maureen Margevanne, Neal Cervera, Shirley Scholsberg, Richard Brookman, Delores Holmes, Judy Snook, Lynn Mullen, Mike Chilver, Russ Mueller, Lawrence Treglia, Sarah York, Georgia Chaffee, and others added immeasurably to my understanding of the needs of families facing the realities of adolescent pregnancy and parenthood.

While most of the photographs are of families which include a teenage parent, the cover photo and several others were staged by photographer Paul Van Dragt. The baby is Travis Rinker, son of Tim Rinker, the book's cover designer. The young "mother" is high school student Danielle Vegter (who is not a teen mother), and the "Grandmother" is Carole Blum. Danielle's mother, Mary Ellen Vegter, modeled for another photo, as did Van Dragt's son, Nicholas. I appreciate their help.

Carole Blum's cover role of grandparent is symbolic of her tireless efforts in editing, proofreading, and keeping me sane throughout the writing of *School-Age Parents*.

Erin B. Lindsay spent many hours editing the manuscript. So did Marie Shaw and Eugenie Wheeler, and I appreciate their help very much.

Bob still manages to be supportive. It takes a strong, loving, and caring man to handle the general commotion created while I'm writing a book, and this is the thirteenth time he has done so. He deserves a medal. He already has my love.

Jeanne Warren Lindsay

Introduction

Grandparents-too-soon is surely an apt description for thousands of parents across the country each year who find themselves expecting a grandchild through their teenage daughter (or son) long before they feel ready to play the grandparenting role. Being a grandparent means rocking the baby and playing with the toddlers *when they come to visit,* not starting all over with live-in infants and toddlers who need constant care. Grandparenting means offering advice occasionally while assuming the child's parents will provide the day-to-day care of that child *and* pay the bills for the inevitable expenses of parenting.

If our children are adolescents, the grandparenting stage may be one we anticipate with joy—but not now, not yet. First we get our children and ourselves through those difficult teen years. Later, when those adolescents are adults, responsible and self-sufficient (translate that to out of the house and into their own homes), *then* the prize at the end of the tunnel is the privilege of playing the grandparent role.

For the parents of pregnant and parenting teenagers, however, the "prize" is now. The baby is here, or anticipated momentarily. Mother is more likely to be single than married, and she probably is not yet financially or emotionally ready to live by herself and take full responsibility for her child. Legally, her parents are responsible for her until her eighteenth birthday. If she becomes pregnant, however, the decision to continue the pregnancy or to have an abortion is hers alone. If she bears the child, the decision of whether to place the baby in an adoptive family or to parent herself is between her and the baby's father. From a legal standpoint, her parents have no voice in these decisions.

If she/they choose to parent the child, however, her (and perhaps his) parents are likely to be deeply involved. There is no way to have a baby in the house without drastic changes occurring in that house.

I talked with hundreds of parents of teenage parents during the sixteen years I coordinated the Teen Mother Program in the ABC Unified School District, Cerritos, California. I visited my students in their homes soon after they learned they were pregnant and heard about the devastation the news had caused for the teenager's parents. I visited after the baby was born and observed the help the young mother often received from her parents. I saw some grandparents become the day-to-day parents of this child born too soon to adolescents not yet ready to parent.

I also knew young parents who received little or no help from their parents, but these were the teenage parents less likely to enroll in our school. Without family support, many dropped out of school and faced futures of poverty and welfare dependence.

On a more positive note, I saw families in which the young mother received the emotional and financial support from her parent(s) which she desperately needed, but who was also allowed to parent her child to the fullest extent possible. It was these families I decided to investigate.

Over the years I observed and kept notes as I visited and talked with these parents of adolescent parents. When I interviewed former teenage parents in preparation for writing *Teens Parenting: The Challenge of Babies and Toddlers,* I was struck by these young mothers' comments concerning their parents' help during their early years of parenting. Over and over I heard, "I couldn't have made it without my parents." And these were the same young mothers who, when their babies were tiny and they were still living at home and attending our classes, would talk about the inevitable frustrations of three-generation living.

In spite of their early start in parenting, these young women were leading successful lives as parents and as individuals. How had they and their parents coped during those early years of becoming parents—or grandparents—too soon?

In addition to the hundreds of home visits with teenage parents and their parents over the years, I interviewed in depth twenty-eight families for this book. They include Anglo, Black and Hispanic families from across the country, families from Florida, Idaho, New York, Kentucky, California, Colorado, and Pennsylvania. The selection is heavily weighted by choice with families who are coping fairly well with the stress of the teenage daughter becoming pregnant, bearing her child, and continuing to live with her parent(s) until she "grows up." Parents of teenage fathers were also interviewed and are quoted, but overwhelmingly it is the young mother and her parents who bear the burden of the day-to-day care and support of the child.

Less than forty percent of teenage mothers are married to the fathers of their babies when the child is born, and many single teenage mothers are not even involved with the fathers of their babies by the time of childbirth. Among the twenty-eight families interviewed, twenty-five percent of the young parents were married, at least for a short time, although the majority of marriages occurred after childbirth.

More than half of the young mothers in this sample were not "with" the baby's father at all at the time of the interviews. Mostly, this book is about young mothers and their parents, about grandparents-too-soon who must cope not only with an adolescent daughter, but with a child for whom they had in no way planned to be responsible.

These grandparents and these teen parents share their stories of lives disrupted, of the pain and the stress caused by this unexpected pregnancy, and of the joy they also experience as parents and grandparents of this wonderful child.

Over and over, the grandparents emphasize the importance of remaining grandparents to the fullest extent possible. Their lives differ from the lives of grandparents whose grandchildren visit only occasionally, but they are still the grandparents, and *not* the parents of this child. The child's mother may be only sixteen, but she is the mother. According to many of these grandparents, their role is to support her, and not to take control of her child.

It's easy to say and it makes sense. But how do you do it? How do you support your teenage daughter as she takes on the role of mother while continuing to some extent the adolescent life so important to her own development? How do you walk that fine line between providing the support she needs but at the same time not filling in as surrogate parents of her child?

This dilemma is, of course, what this book is all about. Grandparents and teenage parents generously share their experiences as they talk about making it through the difficult period of learning about the pregnancy, coping with the months leading up to childbirth, and, even more important, creating a home together for the baby. They talk about the frustrations and disappointments bound to happen, and they suggest ways to work through these inevitable problems.

The names of the families quoted have been changed, and places of residence are not specified in order to protect participants' privacy. A few families were interviewed more than once over a period of two or three years, but most of the interviews occurred in the spring of 1990. Ages given for the teen parents and their babies are accurate, and the quotes, of course, are real. Most of the quotes are from the twenty-eight families interviewed specifically for the book, but some were collected over the years as I worked with teen parents and their families.

Living in a three-generation family caused by the pregnancy of one's teenage daughter is not the life style most of us would choose. It is the life style, however, that many families are living today—families who, when faced with their daughter's unexpected and too-early pregnancy, decided to make it work, to take this unwelcome turn of events and build positive lives for all three of the generations involved.

They are remarkable real-life models for other families facing the crisis of three-generation living.

CHAPTER 1

Not Our Daughter!

When I learned Beth Ann was pregnant, I thought my world was over. We used to hear about people dying of a broken heart, and I was sure my heart was breaking. Peggy Hanley, mother of Beth Ann, pregnant at seventeen.

There's a country song called "Train Wreck of Emotions." That pretty much describes how I felt. For several weeks it was disbelief, shock, anger, all that stuff rolled together. Monica Erickson, mother of Jamie, pregnant at fifteen.

I thought, "There goes my whole life. My whole life is ruined." Veronica Peters, pregnant at fifteen.

My first reaction was anger. I wanted to go kick the crap out of a sixteen-year-old boy, but that wouldn't be a good thing to do. The second thing was to yell at my daughter, but that wasn't the thing to do either—although we did have some heart-to-heart talks. John Adams, father of Colette, pregnant at sixteen.

Nearly 500,000 teenagers give birth each year in the United States, and sixty-one percent of these young women are not married. The pregnancy is a shock to many, and whether or not the young couple is married before the birth, the situation is likely to be difficult for everyone concerned. The young woman and her partner may be confused and scared, while the parents of both the young woman and the young man may be devastated.

Life Plans Change

The girl's parents are facing immediate changes in their lives if their daughter has a baby too soon. She is likely to need their support at this time more than she has ever needed it before. If they are willing to support her, their own lives will change drastically along with hers.

Irene Fletcher, whose daughter, Carole, was pregnant at sixteen, recalled, "We cried together and we shared together. Carole's dad took it a lot harder than I did.

"'Carole,' he said, 'I'm not going to love you any less for this—we all make mistakes—but I had higher goals for you.' Carole is a talented artist, and we thought she'd be going on to college."

Angie Todd was living at home and finishing her first semester of college when she started feeling sick. She missed a lot of classes. When she stayed home one day, her mother took her to the doctor who did a pregnancy test. Angie didn't share the results immediately.

Two days later Angie's mother asked her about her class schedule for the next semester.

"I don't think I'll be going to school."

"You're not?"

"No."

"How come?"

"Because I'm pregnant."

"We both started crying," Angie remembers. "I felt I had ruined every hope Mom had for me. She didn't want me to follow in her footsteps—she had gotten married right out of high school, had a family, put my dad through college, and was now divorced. She thought now I'd do the same thing."

When Do the Parents Find Out?

Over the years, a surprising number of young women have told me their mothers knew they were pregnant before they knew themselves. Several of the women interviewed for this book indicated they realized their daughters were pregnant before they were actually told.

In other families, however, the pregnancy may be kept a secret for an amazingly long time. I talked with one family who didn't know their daughter was pregnant until she went into labor. A few years ago a student enrolled in our school, lived at home with her mother and father throughout her pregnancy, and remained there after her child was born and placed for adoption. *Her father never knew his daughter had been pregnant.* He worked long hours in the business he owned, and, obviously, didn't have much of a relationship with his daughter.

Melissa Baird, seventeen, asked her aunt to be with her while she told her parents, Lorena and Doug. They were horrified, as she had expected. Their initial reaction was that she must get an abortion quickly. Melissa spent that night with her aunt. Her mother said later that was probably a good plan because it gave Doug and her time to get over a little of their shock and anger.

"Melissa had already gone to a Crisis Pregnancy Center, and they had confirmed her feelings about abortion," Lorena explained. "We called the same people and said we needed to talk to someone. They weren't really set up to help parents, but a woman volunteer from the Center came over with her husband, and they spent a Sunday evening with us. Their daughter's baby had been born two months earlier. We found we had a lot in common, and that helped."

While many teenagers say they were "scared to death" when they learned they were pregnant, a surprising number of pregnant and parenting teens tell me they were happy to learn they had conceived. Some think a baby will give them somebody to love and to love them in return. Others think a baby will enhance their relationship with the father. For many, it's simply the excitement a coming baby may trigger for a woman, whatever her age. This doesn't necessarily mean it's easy to tell one's parents about the pregnancy, however.

Alejandra recalled, "I was happy when I found out I was pregnant. At that time, me and the father thought we were in love. It was hard to tell my parents because my mother had helped me get on birth control a few months earlier.

"My parents didn't like my boyfriend so they sent me to Garnett, Kansas, to live with my aunt. I was already pregnant, but I didn't tell them for a couple of months after I got there. I told my dad on the phone.

"My father didn't say anything. In fact, he never talked to me again until I had the baby. But they sent me a plane ticket and I came right home. They didn't want my aunt involved."

Sexual Activity Hard to Accept

Too-early pregnancy may be especially hard on the family with strong religious convictions that premarital sex is absolutely wrong. Their first task may be dealing with the fact that their daughter (or son) is sexually active. The baby probably doesn't seem real at this point. Maggie Hertzel, nineteen, explained:

"When I told them, it was real rough. I come from a strict Catholic family and sex has always been a no-no. That's the way I was brought up.

"When my period was late, I went to the doctor. I was pregnant. How could I tell my parents? That night at 11:30 I went into their room and told them. My dad grumbled and rolled over, and my mom seemed to take it okay. They told me later my dad hadn't said anything because he was so upset.

"We were a very close family, but when this happened, my sister didn't want to have anything to do with me. She was extremely hurt that this had happened to her baby sister."

Maggie and her parents each went to BETA for counseling throughout the rest of Maggie's pregnancy. "My mother was my birth coach, and we actually became friends during my pregnancy," Maggie related. "It was pretty neat having her there."

Baby Due in Two Weeks

Sarah Bradley, seventeen, didn't gain much weight, and her pregnancy didn't "show" through the loose clothes she wore. She tried to pretend she wasn't pregnant, and her parents had no idea throughout the first eight months. Her mother commented, "I guess I had my head tucked in the sand. Several times I asked Sarah if she was pregnant but she always denied it. Finally I said she needed to see the doctor. I made appointments for both of us and took her in because she had never had a pelvic exam before. We learned she was indeed pregnant. She was due in two weeks!

"From the time we found out, Sarah grew phenomenally. It was as if this baby had been waiting for a chance to stretch out.

"Marriage was never considered. We took her to Catholic Social Services for counseling, and they talked about adoption. After several visits there, Sarah knew adoption was not for her."

Sarah's father had hoped his daughter would choose adoption. "She was only seventeen, and I knew it would be rough on her," he said. "What kind of life would the baby have if she kept her? Josie is ten months old now and Sarah still has to depend on us for everything. Of course we love Josie, everybody does, but it's hard for Sarah."

Sarah added, "I denied my pregnancy. I denied it to myself, and I didn't tell my mom. I didn't tell anybody until two or three weeks before I was due. I didn't show that much, but my clothes did fit snugly, and Mom questioned me. It was like I could see my whole life passing me by."

If It's Your Son

Parents whose teenage son has caused a pregnancy may react as strongly as do the parents of the girl. If the young father attempts to shoulder his responsibility, his load may seem impossibly difficult. His parents may see this pregnancy as the end of their dreams for their son's future. Kathleen and Ted Jacobs were proud of their son (they still are) and his future goals. They liked Elsa and saw a lot of her. Both were high school seniors.

"I learned Elsa was pregnant from somebody else," Kathleen recalled. "A friend called and asked how the kids were doing.

"I said, 'Fine.'

"'How are they really doing?'

"'Fine.'

"'Don't you know?'

"'What?'

"'Elsa's pregnant.'

"I started crying. It was April and both were graduating that year.

"Then Ted came home and we started talking. A couple of hours later Lance and Elsa showed up. We asked them what they planned to do. At that point, Elsa didn't want to marry him. She was considering adoption or single parenthood.

"Let's go talk with your parents, Elsa," we said. We called them, and went down that night. All six of us sat down and talked. Elsa's parents had known for some time, and had suggested that the kids not tell us before graduation. They were trying to protect us.

"We visited and talked about who would pay for what. Lance and Elsa had already pretty much figured that out. They would each pay half. Elsa worked as a waitress that summer and Lance as a ranch hand.

"Of course it wasn't this smooth and easy. We were angry, the kids were scared, and so were we . . . and the guilt! I felt a lot of guilt. What in the world did I do wrong? We also felt betrayed. How could these kids do this to us? I would swing back and forth between a wide range of emotions. There was a little joy occasionally, but mostly anger and confusion.

"We got through graduation. My parents came, and I didn't say anything to them. I was terribly afraid to tell my parents for fear they would think I was a bad parent, that I had not done my job."

When/Who Do We Tell?

Many parents find it difficult to share the news of their teenager's pregnancy. They're embarrassed, they feel guilty, and above all, may have always assumed too-early pregnancy happens only to "those girls," and not to their daughter or to their son's girlfriend.

Lois and Don Gray were absolutely devastated when they learned their sixteen-year-old daughter, Robin, was pregnant. "After they calmed down, they became supportive, but for awhile I thought I'd be out on the street," Robin commented. "Those first two months were hard, very hard. Mom started understanding, but my dad kept pushing. 'Why did you do this?' he'd say. I'd made one mistake, and I didn't need my parents on my back."

Don Gray also shared his feelings: "After Robin told me, I just grabbed her and held her. She and I cried together. Then I went into shock, then to anger, and there was a lot of that. I said things I shouldn't have said. We're an ordinary middle-class family, and we thought we had everything together here. We went to church every Sunday, and we were active in the PTA.

"Probably the only good time we had as a family was when the four of us took a two-week vacation to the mountains that summer. After that, everything went a little better."

> *"In spite of our devastation,*
> *we discovered total support*
> *from our friends and our neighbors.*
> *We were amazed."*

Robin's mother added, "There was no consoling my husband for quite a while. He could not believe Robin was pregnant. He even confronted her, and she told him, yes, she was. The first thing we did was find an obstetrician. The second thing we did was have a long talk with our pastor. At first Don and I were so upset, so embarrassed, and we felt so bad. We felt that *everyone* was going to turn their backs on us and think we were awful people and that our daughter was an awful child. Talking to our pastor helped tremendously. We had someone to talk with and to cry with.

"We didn't tell anyone else for months. We didn't tell our parents or any of our family except our children. After a couple of months Don said, 'We've got to tell people.' We told our good friends across the street, and they were supportive. We told a few friends at church, and they were supportive too.

"In spite of our devastation and our belief that everyone
would be down on us, we discovered total support from our
friends, our neighbors, and Robin's friends. We were amazed.
We didn't expect that. So many people we talked with shared,
'This happened to my sister' or 'This happened to my cousin.'"

While families may prefer not to share their problems with
the rest of the world, a baby due to arrive within a few months
(or weeks) is not a keepable secret. No matter how untimely this
pregnancy, if the baby stays in the family, it should be a wanted
baby. A baby deserves to be greeted warmly not only by his
immediate family, but by other caring people.

What Will People Think?

While many parents react with great embarrassment to their
daughter's pregnancy, her partner's parents may also have the
same emotions. When Ronda Grace learned that her seventeen-
year-old son's girlfriend was pregnant, she was shattered. Her
first thought was, "We'll have to leave town." That first day, she
wondered how she could even go grocery shopping. In her mind,
she had failed as a mother, and the whole world would know.

Ronda still doesn't like to talk about the pregnancy. It
shouldn't have happened, and she dreads telling her elderly
father about the coming baby. But Ronda's getting more and
more involved in plans for the baby. With Carlene and Mac's
approval, she has dug out boxes of Mac's baby clothes and is
busily helping the young couple prepare for the baby who will
live with Carlene and her mother.

While Ronda may be unusual in her extreme embarrassment,
many parents feel some of these emotions when they learn of
their teenager's pregnancy. Embarrassment is a very human and
real emotion, but it's not very productive. Trying to focus on
their teenager's predicament, rather than wondering what the
neighbors will think, may help.

Lois Gray commented, "It was hard to walk down the aisle to
communion with Robin after her pregnancy showed. I spent
many a Sunday sitting in church and crying. Actually, Don quit
going to church for awhile, but he's back now. Robin wanted to
go, and that helped me continue.

"Don and I started teaching Sunday school a few months ago because we felt this would be a good outreach for us. It has helped take away some of the hurt we feel by giving ourselves to somebody else, those little ones who give so much to us."

Five months after Roni was born, Don Gray commented, "I'm accepting our situation much better now, probably because of the support our church has provided and the caring we've found in the school's grandparent support group. I'm not down all the time. Here in the neighborhood I can go around the block now with Roni and it doesn't bother me, but I still have problems. Robin will graduate this spring, and she'll go back to her old school for the ceremony. I really don't want to go, and I think Lois feels the same way I do."

Paulette Barrow, whose granddaughter, Teri, is fourteen months old, offers succinct advice concerning "what the neighbors will think."

"Don't give a damn what people think. You have to block this out of your mind. This will change your life. You'll not have the freedom you had, especially if your other children are grown. You may have to give up something.

"There will be good days and there will be bad days. You only hope the good ones outweigh the bad."

Extended Family's Reaction

Parents may be especially concerned about their extended family's reaction. As mentioned earlier, Ronda Grace says she can't tell her elderly father that her son's girlfriend is pregnant. She describes her father as a man who loves babies and children, but she doesn't think he could "stand" the news that his grandson is an unmarried father. Ronda might find reassurance in talking with other families who have faced the same fear.

Kathleen Jacobs, like Ronda, didn't tell her parents her son's girlfriend was pregnant until after Donna was born. Kathleen talked about her mother's reaction:

"My mother put it in perspective. I called her and said, 'I have something awful to tell you,' and I started to cry.

"Mom said, 'What is it?'

"I said, 'Lance and Elsa have a baby.'

"'Oh my goodness, I thought you were going to tell me
something terrible like somebody is sick,' she responded. She
put it in perspective. That's an awful fear, wondering what
you're going to hear from your parents, and how you're going to
get nailed."

Sarah Bradley's father, Walker, who didn't know his daughter
was pregnant until two weeks before she delivered, had to share
the news with his relatives:

"No one in our family came down on her and said she was
bad. Not even my mother, and she is very good at opening her
mouth. I called her and said, 'I have something to tell you, but if
you're going to yell and scream, I don't want to talk to you.' She
said she'd be quiet. We went up there and told her, and it's the
first time I've heard my mama keep her mouth shut."

"I Can't Handle Another Baby"

In some families, adding a baby to the household seems
utterly impossible to the parents. Lacy Dillen's daughter enrolled briefly in our Teen Mother Program. Lacy had called me
the day before because she wanted to talk. She was extremely
upset and said, among other things, "I won't tolerate another
child in my house. I don't know whether Sandy is doing this for
spite—she had the pill. I don't know what's wrong, I don't
know. She's so messed up, and I have been told I'm responsible
for her until she's eighteen.

"I talked to a volunteer counselor at a Crisis Center," Lacy
continued, "who screamed at me and told me I was a no-good
mother, but I won't have Sandy's baby in my home. I just can't.
As much as I want my daughter, I will not go through having
another baby. I had one all by myself, and that one was Sandy.
I don't know what's going to happen."

Three days after Sandy enrolled in the Teen Mother Program,
she was gone, a runaway. We heard she and her boyfriend had
gone to another state to live, but we had no way to contact them.
While one may understand this mother's strong feelings, her
daughter is not likely to do well without her mother's support.
Sandy's boyfriend, according to her mother, is on drugs and
can't hold a job. Sandy's future doesn't look promising.

Jessica and Lee Williams felt perhaps as negative toward their daughter's pregnancy as did Lacy. However, they realized how much Arlana, sixteen and pregnant, needed their support, although they didn't know at first whether they could provide that support.

"It's hard to keep our emotions out of it,
and it gets right in the middle
of our marriage."

About two months before the baby was due, Lee explained, "Our first vision was that we would end up with this little baby as so many grandparents do. It's hard to keep our emotions out of it, and it gets right in the middle of our marriage. We haven't talked very well between ourselves. We enjoyed our marriage a lot before we had children, and we were looking forward to the no-child time. We both see this as a tremendous threat to our future plans.

"I don't think we were particularly embarrassed, but we were crushed at the effect this would have on Arlana's future."

Lee talked about the need for parents to help their daughter understand the choices she has, and he emphasized that it has to be her decision. There is no easy decision, and *she must know it is hers, not anyone else's.*

"Jessica and I don't really agree," Lee continued. "Jessica doesn't want a baby in this house. I'm more reserved with my advice to Arlana, and I'm almost paranoid about Jessica making the decision rather than Arlana. Any time we talk about it, we end up in the same position.

"I agree that adoption would solve some of the problems, but there are some perils there. I think Jessica knows that, but she is so distraught about having a young child in the house again. That's just not in our plans, and we know that would be hard on both of us, but harder on Jessica.

"If Arlana keeps the baby, we have almost decided that after a short time at home, we would find her some place else to live, although we really can't afford it. We have said this to Arlana. In fact, at first we were so firm about it that she thought after the baby is born, we'd kick her out immediately. She was desperately searching for a place to live, and we assured her she could stay here for awhile. But there has to be some sort of limit. Otherwise the status quo could continue forever.

"Jessica is upset with Arlana because she took our future and tore it up," Lee concluded.

Stages of Grief

People grieving the loss of a loved one *or* another significant loss usually proceed through several stages of grief including shock, denial, anger, and depression as they work toward acceptance of their loss.

A daughter's too-early pregnancy is likely to bring on these stages of grieving for both the grandparents and the daughter. The daughter may not acknowledge her grief over the loss, in many ways, of her teenage years, although some teenage mothers describe their feelings in this way.

Her parents also grieve for their daughter's loss, and they grieve for their own loss. Part of their loss is that they are not becoming grandparents in the traditional way and at the traditional time.

Shock is usually the first stage of grief, and parents often describe their feelings of deep shock when they first learn their teenage daughter is pregnant. Shock often turns into denial. "This can't be happening to *our* family."

Shock and denial may change to anger. "How dare our daughter do this to us?" You may have a strong desire to hurt your daughter's partner for what he has done to her and to your entire family.

Parents also talk about the guilt they feel. "What should we have done or not done so this wouldn't happen?"

Depression is likely to hit after you can no longer deny this pregnancy. Your anger has diminished and you realize, whether it's your fault or not, it's happening.

Acceptance is the ultimate goal in grieving. "This is happening. What do we do now? We can't change the fact that a baby is coming." If she decides to parent her child, how can you help her become the parent your grandchild will need?

Jessica Williams, who works with parents who have mis-carried or given birth to a stillborn baby, attended a workshop on grieving two years after Arlana's baby was born. As she listened to a description of these stages of grief, Jessica, to her surprise, recognized them. She had experienced them herself as she coped first with Arlana's pregnancy, and then with the difficult realities of three-generation living.

"I didn't put it all together at the time, but I remember going through all those stages," she related. "It takes a long time to get to the acceptance stage. For me, it wasn't a straight route. I'd go back and forth with the anger and the depression, anger at her partner for doing this to us, and depression because of these changes we hadn't anticipated for our family.

"It helps me to understand these stages, and to know that acceptance will happen. It just takes awhile," she concluded.

Jean Brunelli, who works with the parents of handicapped babies and toddlers in the Tracy Infant Center, Cerritos, California, concurs:

"The parents of handicapped infants grieve the death of a dream," she commented, "and so do the parents of pregnant teens. They, too, are losing a dream as they see their child become a parent, and themselves grandparents, before any of them are ready."

Dealing with the Crisis

Neal Cervera, Ph.D., co-leader of a grandparent support group in Albany, New York, points out that before parents or their teens can deal with the crisis of too-early pregnancy, they have to get over their "Oh my God, my daughter is pregnant" or "My son has gotten someone pregnant" stage. Then they must deal with the issue of denial or avoidance, and they may have trouble accepting the fact that their teenage daughter or son is sexually active.

"You have to acknowledge to yourself that you have lost con-trol," he emphasized. "Your daughter has the decision-making responsibility now. It is she who decides whether to continue her pregnancy, it is she and her partner who must make the adoption/keeping decision. Parents can provide input, but by law they have lost control. At the same time, parents face the double whammy of being financially responsible for the pregnancy."

Sometimes the pregnancy helps family members become closer to one another, according to Cervera. In other families, it makes things worse. How they have solved problems in the past will affect their approach to this problem.

"Parents need to know this is a crisis, but it is also an opportunity," Cervera continued. "Their feelings are real, and they need to appreciate those feelings of hurt and sadness and despair. Initially they may feel strong guilt. 'Where did we go wrong?' 'I shouldn't have let her go out with him.' These feelings need to be acknowledged. The next step is realizing the parents couldn't stop the pregnancy. It is *not* their fault.

"An important step in acknowledging your feelings and dealing with your exasperation is to say, 'Is there anyone in my community I can lean on?' Keeping a pregnancy a secret is not realistic. Even if you send her to Ohio, how will you respond to your neighbors? To your relatives? You need to lean on friends, neighbors, church, other support people. Can someone help you who has gone through this?

"Ask your daughter about her future goals. What does she want for herself and her baby? If she is planning to stay home, where is the money going to come from for a crib, diapers, formula, pediatric care?" Cervera asked.

"Show That You Care"

If you are a pregnant teen or the partner of a pregnant teen, what do you want from your parents? Raelynn Barrow, single and pregnant at twenty-one, put it succinctly:

"Show that you care. The best thing for me is knowing my parents are here for me even though I have goofed up. They still love me and they let me know that. My biggest fear when I was deciding what to do . . . I just couldn't bear the thought of my parents not wanting me around."

CHAPTER 2

Coping
With Pregnancy

I stayed with her during a long and active labor. "I don't believe I'm doing this. I don't believe it," I kept thinking. Her baby was born, and our lives were changed forever. Jessica Williams, mother of Arlana, pregnant at sixteen.

If I could advise parents, I'd say they need to give us our space. You need to grow yourself rather than having someone there pushing you. You have to make your own mistakes in order to grow. Melissa, pregnant at seventeen.

"If you keep this baby, it's yours to feed, to change, to get up with at night," I told her. We put all the baby paraphernalia in Angie's room. Angie had one-hundred-percent care of Rachel. I was there as the older experienced person, but I didn't hop up to heat bottles. Anita Nolan, mother of Angie, pregnant at seventeen.

Medical Care Is Crucial

If your teenager is pregnant, her health and her baby's health
are of primary importance. If she has not told anyone she's
pregnant until now, she probably has not gotten medical care.
Once she decides to continue her pregnancy, she needs to see a
doctor, and she needs to see that doctor regularly throughout her
pregnancy. A teenager who receives excellent and regular
prenatal care is much less likely to have health problems during
her pregnancy or to deliver her baby too soon.

Parents may need time to recover from their teenage
daughter's pregnancy announcement, but as soon as possible
they should get her to an obstetrician or a midwife. Check to see
if your hospital or clinic has special services for adolescents. In
some communities, these services include extra counseling and
intensive guidance on nutrition and other prenatal health issues.

Ideally, a woman would have a complete physical exam
before she conceives, and she would see her doctor regularly
throughout her pregnancy. She would drink no alcohol, she
would not smoke, and she wouldn't take drugs immediately
before or during her pregnancy. She would eat nutritious foods
all during this time.

Teenagers are at higher risk for premature birth and other
problems during pregnancy. However, those teens at least
sixteen years old who eat well, see their doctors regularly, and
do not drink alcohol, smoke, or take drugs probably are at no
greater physical risk than are pregnant women in their twenties.
The importance of adequate prenatal care for pregnant teenagers
is great.

Sometimes a family medical plan covers an unmarried
daughter's pregnancy and delivery, but does not provide health
insurance for the baby. Some insurance plans cover both mother
and baby, and some provide no help at all with this pregnancy.
If your daughter's pregnancy and/or child are not covered by
private insurance, you can check with your Department of
Social Services, or ask the doctor or hospital where to go for
information concerning financial aid.

As soon as Monica Erickson learned her daughter was pregnant, she called the doctor. She recalled, "The first thing was

medical attention. In the beginning, we didn't talk about who would be responsible for the baby because I thought Jamie should consider adoption. I was pretty convinced she was too young to be a mother. I told her she was too young to parent and I was too old. She needed to think about adoption.

"We took it one step at a time. Jamie got into a teen pregnancy program at our hospital. She saw a midwife throughout her pregnancy, and a social worker was always available.

"Until she made the decision to keep her baby, we didn't talk about arrangements for her child. My major concerns were medical coverage for the baby and daycare. Both Toby and I have health insurance through our jobs, and Jamie is covered by both policies, but neither policy would cover her baby.

"We have six children and Jamie is the youngest. We already had four grandchildren, and the baby clothes started coming in from those families. So that was covered.

"About two weeks before the baby was born, we were ready. We had taken care of the practical things. We had a crib and clothes, and we had a supply of diapers. By that time, I could hardly wait. I didn't want to deal with a pregnant daughter any longer. I needed something different. I felt saturated."

Prenatal Nutrition Important to Baby

Teenagers tend to have poor nutrition habits. A non-pregnant teen may be able to cope with french fries and a coke for lunch, but if she's pregnant, that kind of diet won't do. In fact, changes in eating may be the biggest life style change she needs to make during her pregnancy.

The March of Dimes Birth Defects Foundation has a wonderful and inexpensive filmstrip titled "Inside My Mom" which offers a delightful way to learn about nutrition during pregnancy. Call your local MOD chapter for information.

A teen may have at least two reasons for not eating properly during pregnancy. She may not want to—just as most of us prefer to eat what we like rather than constantly worrying about what's good for us. The second reason could be that she doesn't find much nutritious food at home. Some parents don't feel they can afford the extra milk a pregnant teen needs daily. Enrolling

in WIC (Women, Infant and Children food program) at the local
health department makes her eligible for coupons for milk and
other nutritious foods during pregnancy. WIC is designed for
high-risk women and children, and a young teen, by virtue of
being pregnant, is generally considered high risk.

In some families, the majority of meals are eaten at fast food
places. If this is the case, the family might learn which fast foods
are most desirable from a nutrition standpoint. Perhaps the
parents will be able to set a good example for their pregnant
daughter.

If she eats out with her boyfriend, he needs to know about
nutrition needs during pregnancy. Perhaps he'll demonstrate his
support by eating these foods with her. (He might be surprised at
the increase in energy this could give him.)

Nine months may seem like an eternity to eat foods which
aren't necessarily one's favorites. However, what the mother
eats during this time can have a tremendous influence on her
baby's future health.

I've often been amazed at the changes in eating habits of
many of the pregnant students in our Teen Mother Program. If a
new student brings a coke, another student is likely to say,
"Drink your milk. That coke isn't good for your baby." Almost
all of our students stop smoking when they learn they're
pregnant. What a wonderful gift to give one's baby!

Where Will She Live?

In the past, many pregnant teenagers were sent either to live
with Aunt Matilda in Milwaukee or to a maternity home during
the last few months before delivery. This often tied in with the
adoption decision and the assumption that the young mother
would then go home, no one would know she had been
pregnant, and she would forget the whole experience.

Of course this didn't happen. She never forgot either her baby
or the experience of being pregnant too soon.

Today, for some young women, living some place other than
with their parents may still be a good decision, especially if
tension within the family is extremely high. A good maternity
home may offer excellent counseling and other services needed

by the young woman. Or she and her parents may choose a private home set up to serve pregnant teens.

Heidi Winters ran away from home when she was fifteen. She was gone six weeks, and when she came home, she was pregnant. She was ordered by the court to live in a local maternity home and attend school there. Her father, Jack Winters, recalls, "That was a blessing because we were at our wit's end. Living at BETA was a good growing process for her. I was feeling a lot of anger and frustration at that time, so the separation was good for me, too.

> *"Our basic rule was,*
> *'This is your child*
> *and you must care for it.'"*

"We were counseled as a family and separately. At first, I assumed Heidi would release her baby for adoption. I wasn't going to allow her to come home with this baby. Then I learned this was not my decision. Only she could decide whether or not she would keep her baby. She let us think she was planning adoption for several months, then in her last month, she told us she would parent her child.

"We allowed her to come home with her baby. Our basic rule was, 'This is your child, and you must care for it.' We were financially strapped, and I didn't know how I could feed my family, let alone her baby. Heidi got a job at McDonald's, and we gave her a roof over her head.

"There were problems. Heidi keeps a lot of her feelings inside, and sometimes it's tough to talk with her."

The decision to leave home during pregnancy needs to be based on a thorough study of the possibilities. Hopefully, parents and daughter will agree on the decision.

Many families today feel that sending their daughter away during this extremely stressful stage of her life is not wise, and perhaps not even loving. She may need her parents now more than she ever has.

Several teens interviewed for this book had been away from home for several months, at least two as runaways. Coming back

home would be difficult in any case, but being pregnant and
returning home created special challenges for these young
women and their parents.

Back Home Again

Melissa's pregnancy was a real shock to her upper middle-
class parents, Lorena and Doug Baird. Lorena and Doug felt
Melissa should live elsewhere during her pregnancy. Rather than
going to a maternity home, Melissa went with Pete to spend the
summer in Kentucky with Pete's grandmother. That was a tough
time, especially for Melissa.

"I was sick the first five months, and it was awful moving in
with Pete's family," she recalled. "I did the basic things like
clean our room and the bathroom, but his grandma wanted me
to do more—except she'd never tell me what she wanted.

"There were a lot of problems there—screaming fits. The
other relatives thought I was after Pete. This was the first time
I had ever met them, and they thought I was giving Pete
a problem.

"I got through the summer by not saying anything. I'd walk
away. I tried to stay out of it as much as possible, and even that
bothered Pete's grandmother. She wouldn't say anything to me.
She'd go to Pete, which was part of the problem. If she had a
problem with me, she should have come to me in the first place.

"This caused a lot of fights between Pete and me. I'd tell him
I was leaving, that I'd walk to the airport. Finally I called Mom
and said, 'Come get me. Send me an airline ticket.'

"We both went back to my home, and a lot of things had
changed. My mom got Pete a job, and she helped me enroll in a
teen parent program at school. Mom and Dad's attitude had
changed a lot while I was gone. They were much more positive,
and I tried to make it as easy on them as I could. I was at school
every day. I kept my room neat. As long as you take care of
yourself, pick up after yourself, my mom's fine.

"I was five months pregnant when I came back, and I hadn't
been to a doctor. My mom got me an appointment immediately."

Pete talked about the job Melissa's mother got for him. "I was
learning to operate a fork lift, and I didn't like it," he said, "but I

really had no choice. I'm still doing that, and I'm used to it now. When I started, I'd come home dead tired, and I'd take my frustrations out on Melissa. I wanted to quit that job but . . ."

Melissa interjected, "We'd fight a lot. My parents would get in the middle of our fights and try to settle things down. We'd get lectures almost every night. They didn't take anybody's side. They just wanted to be mediators.

"If I could advise parents, I'd say they need to give kids their space. You need to grow yourself rather than having someone there pushing you. You have to do it your way. You have to make your own mistakes in order to grow. My parents don't want us to make mistakes so they say, 'You have to do this . . .'"

Lorena and Doug agreed that having Melissa and Pete away for the summer was a good strategy. "We needed time to re-group," Lorena said. "We weren't being mean to Melissa, but we needed time apart. When they came back, we helped."

When asked how they handled all this, Doug replied, "With brute force and awkwardness. It was a tough period."

Making the Big Decision

Sometimes the period of pregnancy goes well. The teen and her mother may find they feel closer than ever to one another. While it may be easier to let the time slip away during these months without doing much planning for the future, it's unwise to do so. What is being planned for the baby? Will it be an adoption plan or a parenting plan? Less then five percent of pregnant teenagers carry out an adoption plan, but too often, no real parenting plan is made. Parenting almost seems to happen by default.

Adoption agencies and independent adoption counseling centers almost never assume their clients plan adoption. In fact, if the agency or independent adoption center counselors suggest their clients "should" release their babies, its counseling system is questionable. That agency/center probably should be avoided.

Instead, a good counselor, whether with an adoption agency, independent adoption center, or other source, will focus on the needs of the client. What are the pros and cons of keeping her baby? Of releasing for adoption? If you choose adoption, how open do you want the process to be? If she parents the child herself, where will she live? How will she continue her education? Does she have a financial plan?

The counselor's goal is not to convince the client that she "should" place for adoption or that she "should" parent her child herself. The goal is to help the client make the best possible decision for herself and her child.

Several books are available to help with the adoption/parenting decision-making, such as *Pregnant Too Soon: Adoption Is an Option*, written for birthparents; *Open Adoption: A Caring Option*, an explanation and examples of the kind of adoption where the birthparents and the adoptive parents meet and may continue contact after the adoption is finalized; *Parents, Pregnant Teens and the Adoption Option: Help for Families*, for birthgrandparents—the parents of pregnant teens considering adoption; and *Adoption Awareness: A Guide for Teachers, Counselors, Nurses, and Caring Others*, for professionals and other helping persons. These books are published by Morning Glory Press.

She's been there for both decisions—
adoption and keeping.

Heidi Winters looks at the adoption/keeping decision from a different perspective than most people. She's been there for both decisions—adoption and keeping.

Heidi's first baby was born when she was fifteen. Her parents insisted she consider adoption, so she talked with a counselor. Early on, however, Heidi told the counselor and her parents that she definitely wanted to parent her baby herself.

A year later, Heidi was pregnant again by her first baby's father. This time, her parents were outspoken about not having two babies in their home. This time, Heidi carried out an adoption plan. The aftermath of neither her parenting nor her adoption decision has been easy for Heidi. Holidays are especially difficult, she says.

Heidi frequently talks to pregnant teenagers in the throes of decision-making. She commented, "When I was pregnant, my parents said they would go along with whatever decision I made. I've seen a lot of girls whose parents want them to keep this baby 'because this is my grandchild.' They say, 'Keep it, keep it.' I don't think that's right. The parents should go along with whatever decision she makes.

"Now, because I'm parenting my first baby and I released the other one to another family, I know what it's like both ways. It's hard for a first-time pregnant teen to think about adoption. When it's your first baby, you don't want to lose that baby.

"But now that I have gone through both, I can tell them what it's like to release and what it's like to keep.

"Recently I talked with a fifteen-year-old, and we talked about both options. I told her both sides. If I could go back four or five years, I said, I'd probably look at adoption more closely the first time. Everything changes, whichever way you go."

What About Baby's Father?

If your daughter and her boyfriend are still together, how much will they see each other? Does making a baby together mean they should be together as much as possible, perhaps live together? Or does it mean she's not allowed to communicate with him at all? The situation varies from family to family, and of course the situation also varies considerably from boyfriend to boyfriend.

If the baby's father is no longer involved with the young mother, decisions must still be made concerning his contact with the baby and the financial support he will provide. If an adoption plan is made, his signature will be needed for the adoption papers.

If the parents feel this young man is absolutely no good for their daughter, what should they do? Refer to chapter four for suggestions from families facing this situation.

On the other hand, if the parents feel marriage is in order because of the pregnancy, how much should they push? Generally, the marriage decision should be made as separately from the pregnancy as possible. Many pregnant teens have wisely told me, "Getting married because I'm pregnant wouldn't work. Two wrongs don't make a right." This can be a difficult concept for

parents who feel strongly that marriage is a necessary part of
having children. If the young couple would marry quickly, they
hope, the problem might vanish.

If the young couple is considering marriage or moving in
together, *Teenage Marriage: Coping with Reality* (1988:
Morning Glory Press) is a helpful resource.

Day-to-Day Decisions

In addition to getting medical care and making all these
crucial decisions, practical tasks must be considered. If adoption
is not the choice, where will the baby sleep? Will the young
mother breastfeed or bottle feed? Will she continue in school? Is
there childcare at her school? Must she get a job to support her
baby? What about childcare while she's working?

Who will actually care for the baby, get up at night, feed him,
change him, rock him, take care of him when he's sick? Most of
us would agree that ideally the young parent will take care of her
child. She needs to bond with her child, and the child needs to
be very sure exactly which woman in the household is his
mother and which one is his grandmother.

Young parents and their parents need to communicate their
needs clearly to each other. Preferably before the baby is born,
they need to talk about how much babysitting the grandparents
are willing to do. Will the teen parent go out every Friday
night—or every night—and expect her parents to babysit? See
suggestions for a family contract in chapter eight.

Most of the grandparents interviewed resented being *expected*
to babysit. If their daughter asked them, then truly accepted their
"No" as well as their "Yes" answers, there was less resentment.
Everyone likes being appreciated, and grandparents who are
expected to babysit with no thanks in return are more likely to
resent the whole process.

While these decisions are being made, the day-to-day needs
of the coming baby must be considered. "Carole got the little
bed ready," Irene Fletcher explained. "The bathinette I had used
for Carole was still in the attic, and we brought that down. I
painted it and her dad put vinyl covering on the top. Our other
daughter had an extra chest of drawers which Carole painted.

Her boyfriend gave her some money to buy things for the baby, and we went shopping. Carole's child development teacher helped her figure out what she needed.

"Carole shares a fairly big room with her little sister. Because Carole wanted some privacy, she and her father put a curtain up in the middle of the room. Actually, Carole did pretty well at getting things ready for the baby."

Concrete Stage of Thinking

In our school's Teen Mother Program, we teach a daily prenatal health class and two daily parenting classes, one for parents of infants, and the other for parents of toddlers. When I ask each class to discuss the challenge of three-generation living, the differences from class to class are more revealing than the differences from individual to individual.

Teen parents of toddlers talk a lot about the problems of living with their parents. They don't want their parents to tell them how to raise their babies. They are still teenagers, and tend to rebel against their parents just as non-parenting teenagers do.

Parents of infants, however, tend to appreciate the help their mothers provide. At least during the first couple of months, they are unsure of their parenting skills, want to be good parents, and probably will accept some advice from their mothers.

In the prenatal health class, however, reality has not yet hit, and one is most likely to hear, "Everything will be OK."

"My mom tells me it will be hard, but I don't think so."

"It will bring our family closer together. My sisters and I hardly know each other any more. The baby will get us talking."

"I'll take responsibility for everything by buying things . . . but I won't be working."

"I'll be living with my mother. It might be a little hard, but my mother will help out."

These young women are typical teenagers. Looking ahead realistically is almost impossible. It's not because they're stupid. Rather, this is one of the characteristics of adolescent development, the living-for-the-moment mindset. Making plans for next week is difficult, and planning for the next eighteen years is virtually impossible for most teenagers.

Laverne Grahek's daughter, Lydia, is pregnant. Laverne commented, "Lydia has some plans that I think are mostly unrealistic. She talks about working, going to school, and taking care of the baby. I don't know how she expects to do all these things. She doesn't have any clear-cut plans. She'll have to experience the reality of having a baby before she can have any clear idea of what she's talking about."

So what is a parent to do? How do you nudge your fifteen-year-old to a different level of thinking which is more future-oriented? How will she respond to her baby, and to her new life as a parent? How can you begin to help her understand the enormous changes she'll be facing?

Fred Grahek, Lydia's father, says this starts with the parents' feelings. He stated firmly, "The biggest thing I've been trying to do is help my wife realize this isn't her baby, and to make Lydia realize this will be her child. We'll be supportive, but we already have five children, and we aren't doing that again.

"We'll have to take a step back and not take over. Lydia needs to mature, and that's a real struggle. Her mother and I have to realize we can't map it all out and plan every minute, because this problem isn't ours. I don't think it would be right for us to become responsible for this baby. We don't want to parent an infant again.

"We're trying hard to help Lydia become aware of what will happen once the baby is here, but it's a frustrating task."

Life Goes On

Will house rules change for the teenager now that she's pregnant? Sometimes parents go to one of two extremes. Perhaps from feelings of embarrassment, they attempt to keep their daughter at home as much as possible. Or at the other extreme, they reduce their rules considerably now that their daughter is old enough to have a baby. Probably the happy medium is to encourage her to lead as normal a life as possible considering the circumstances. At the same time, she needs to make realistic plans for herself and her baby.

Angie Nolan didn't go out much while she was pregnant. Her boyfriend seemed to be embarrassed to be seen with her which hurt Angie a lot. She wasn't doing the things normal teenagers do. So a number of times at 8 p.m. on Friday, her mother would say, "I'm going to the mall. Does anyone want to go with me?" Often Angie would tag along.

"I'd deliberately look for someplace to go, thinking Angie might want to come along, just to get her out of the house," Anita said. "She never knew I was doing it for that reason, and she would always go. But none of her friends invited her out."

Siblings Affected

Sometimes older siblings are upset by their sister's too-early pregnancy. Perhaps they feel this is ruining their little sister's life, and they wanted more for her. Or they may be embarrassed as she looks more and more pregnant. Colette Adams, pregnant at sixteen, found this so difficult she was delighted when her sister moved out:

"Betty was very upset that I was pregnant," Colette related. "Of course she never admitted it, but I think she was jealous.

"She strongly, strongly encouraged me to place the baby for adoption. At times she was downright mean. She was angry, and she would say mean things to me. She'd been away at college for two years and had recently returned home. And coming home to a pregnant sixteen-year-old sister was not what she had in mind.

"My parents got upset when they heard her nasty remarks to me, but most of the time they weren't aware of all this.

"My sister had her room and I had mine, and rearranging everyone to accommodate a new baby was hard. My mom and dad had an office downstairs in a little bedroom. They moved their stuff out and had Betty move down there to make room for Marisa in the room next to mine. My sister moved out about a month later. Once she was gone, the space tension was eased. I was glad to get rid of her."

Erin Williams, Arlana's sister, remembers feeling some resentment after her younger sister's baby was born. "Penny is a wonderful child, but I was the one who had a car, so I had to take Arlana and Penny to the doctor. My mother and I also had to take care of Penny when Arlana got an evening job. I didn't mind the mess as much as my mother did, but tripping over the toys and the diapers wasn't fun!

"My sister and I have always been competitive, and I remember feeling jealous when Arlana got all that attention while she was pregnant and after Penny was born," Erin continued. "I was jealous, too, of the fact that my parents were supporting her while she didn't work those first six months, and I had to go out and get a job."

Younger siblings, too, may have trouble dealing with their sister's pregnancy. Sara York is the Family Programs Coordinator for the Teenage Parent Program (TAPP), Jefferson County, Kentucky, Public Schools. "Because of the pressures our students' siblings are feeling, we developed a program to help younger sisters and brothers aged six to sixteen deal with their feelings of jealousy, anger, and resentment," York explained.

"We teach them alternative ways to be successful, and we show them you don't have to have a baby to gain people's attention and love. We do a lot of self-esteem building projects, and we work closely with their school counselors in helping siblings with their special problems," York concluded.

Parents already overwhelmed with a daughter's pregnancy need also to deal with their other children's needs. It's not easy.

Attend School During Pregnancy

School attendance is all-important for pregnant teenagers. In fact, it's probably even more important that a pregnant or parenting teen finish school on time than it is for her non-pregnant peers. A young mother needs to get on with her life. One of the more irrational things done in the past was to push young women out of school because of pregnancy, whether married or not.

For nearly two decades it has not been legal to push a student out of public school for any of these reasons, and if a private school receives funding from the federal government, the same rules probably apply. However, this still happens in some school districts.

If you (or your daughter) is told a pregnant girl cannot stay in regular classes, call your school district office and ask to speak to the Title IX supervisor. If you don't get help there, go to your county Office of Education to report this violation of the law.

It's not even legal to force a pregnant student to attend special classes for pregnant teens. However, if your district provides such classes, find out about them. Talk to the teacher and visit the school. Many of these programs are excellent and can offer some of the special services not available in many schools. In addition, and perhaps most important, the students offer each other support at a time in their lives when their former friends are just that, *former* friends.

Pregnancy generally does not qualify as sufficient reason for home teaching.

Rich and Elaine Wright's daughter, Charlene, fifteen, is five months pregnant, and the Wrights felt a strong sense of shame when they learned this had happened. They pulled Charlene out of school immediately and insisted on a home teacher. (In most schools, home teachers are available only for students too disabled to get to school. Pregnancy generally does not qualify as sufficient reason for home teaching.)

The Wrights live in a school district which offers a special class, a Teen Mother Program, as a choice for pregnant students. If Charlene doesn't want to continue in her regular classes throughout her pregnancy, she probably would gain more from attending the special program than she would from home teaching. Not only would she participate in special prenatal health and prepared childbirth activities in addition to continuing her academic studies, but, and perhaps most important, she would have the support of other young women in similar situations.

As a teacher in a public school Teen Mother Program, time after time I have watched a young woman enroll who appeared to be depressed and to have low self-esteem. To her, only "those girls" get pregnant, yet here she was. She must be a bad person.

As she became acquainted with other girls in the class, however, she soon realized that these were "nice" girls too, girls who were working hard at coping with their situations. Perhaps she could cope, too.

A few schools for pregnant teens even offer support groups for students' parents. (See chapter seven.) If Rich and Elaine could find such a group, they might find comfort in learning how other families deal with their daughter's too-early pregnancy.

Stacy Bloom is married now and has three children. The father of her first child split when he learned Stacy, a high school junior, was pregnant, and Stacy lived with her parents for three years. She feels offering information about her school's Teen Mother Program to her mother at the same time she told her mom she was pregnant helped soften the blow.

Elena Stoltz, fifteen, and her mother, Adele, went together to see Elena's counselor and to check Elena out of the comprehensive high school and into the district's Teen Mother Program. "Our next step was to check out the special school program," Adele said. "My husband and I went over there first. It's not located in a very good area, and I saw girls there who didn't look like our daughter. Some appeared ready to deliver, and perhaps I hadn't accepted that stage yet. When I left there, I was crying. The place looked awful to me, and I didn't want her to enroll in that program.

"Elena didn't want to return to her home school, so I enrolled her in the special school. Once we made that decision, it seemed we could handle the pregnancy. I could say 'baby' without crying.

"The school worked out great. Elena's happy there; she has made some wonderful friends. She gets a lot of private tutoring and her grades have improved. I think she feels at home there. My initial reaction to the school doesn't make sense to me now."

Prepared Childbirth Class

Labor and delivery will probably go better for your daughter if she takes prepared childbirth classes during her last two or three months of pregnancy. These classes are available from private instructors in most areas, at many hospitals, and through adult education in many school districts. Some private teachers are rather expensive, but adult education classes may require only a small fee.

To enroll in the classes, she must have a coach. If the baby's father is involved, fine. If not, who might volunteer? A friend? Sister? Mother? Father? Arlana Williams, in spite of some extremely difficult times in her relationship with her mother, asked her mom to attend the classes with her.

Jessica recalls, "I told Arlana I would go to Lamaze classes with her, so she signed up, and off we went.

"Arlana didn't seem bothered by the yuppie couples, and she made an immediate hit with the instructor. We managed to get through those classes.

"She had a lot of false labor. Then she woke me one night at 1 a.m. 'This is the real thing.' We called the doctor, and I took her in at 4 a.m. I stayed with her during a long and active labor. 'I don't believe I'm doing this. I don't believe it,' I kept thinking.

"Her baby was born, and our lives were changed forever."

As she talked, a year later, Jessica's voice broke. "I never thought all that hurt was still here, but it's very painful even today," she admitted.

Clarification of Roles Is Important

Clarification of roles is of primary importance, according to Delores Holmes, Director of Our Place, Family Focus, Evanston, Illinois. While most of the families interviewed for this book stress the value of the teenager taking over completely the role of mother to her baby, Holmes sees this not happening in some families. Sometimes the mother is simply considered too young and immature to care for her child herself, and her mother may feel she needs to take over as parent to her daughter's baby.

"They need to make sure the teen mother is in agreement with the grandmother playing mother," Holmes stresses. "Then the grandmother needs to assume all the parenting responsibilities. I say this because the grandmother will often take on the role of mothering the baby up to a point. Then when she doesn't want to do it, she gives the baby back to the mother. Often this is done as punishment. The teen mother can't take the baby places, has no say in decision-making, but when the grandmother gets tired, it's the teen's baby. They have to clarify their roles."

Holmes also points out the difficulties faced by the grandparent who is responsible for her own child, the teen mother, but
has no real say in decisions about the welfare of her daughter's
child. "That, too, creates a lot of dissension," Holmes observed.
"When the teen mother assumes the major parenting role but
she can't assume the financial responsibility, it gets out of
balance again."

Maintaining Relationships Stressed

Martha and Brian Simpson, parents of Amy, pregnant at
seventeen, offered advice to other parents coping with their
daughter's too-early pregnancy:

"First of all, Mom and Dad have to get their heads together
because a pregnant daughter can certainly strain their relationship," Brian pointed out. "The pregnancy may be a problem, it
may seem to be tragic, but you don't want it to ruin the relationship between the two of you.

"If you have any religion, go see your clergy," Brian added.
"He opened my eyes. We weren't there very long, but he helped
us a lot by pointing out a different perspective on the whole
situation."

"Amy stayed close to us," Martha said. "I think it would be
terrible if you had that separation, and she wouldn't come
around. We're a close-knit family from the grandparents on
down, and if she pulled away, it would have been even harder.

"I don't think a day goes by that my heart doesn't ache,"
Martha continued. "Sometimes I want to cry, but I try to teach
my children to look at the positive side. And of course Erica is
the positive thing in all this. She's our pride and joy."

Getting through a teenager's too-early pregnancy is seldom
easy for anyone. It is a time of grieving, of shock, denial, and
often anger. It is also a time to deal with reality, to plan for the
coming baby. With lots of love, respect, and caring, many
families manage to maintain, perhaps even improve their
relationships with each other during this crucial time. This is
indeed a challenge.

CHAPTER **3**

For Dad
(Grandpa)

The hardest part is when you first find out. Your world is shattered, everything you've worked for. You're hit hard. I felt like my daughter had betrayed me. Jerry Hertzel, father of Maggie, pregnant at nineteen.

Her father had difficulty looking at her and talking with her. I wanted to lean on him, but he wouldn't let me because this was more than he could take. He had to lean on me. Sylvia Hertzel, Jerry's wife.

Dad don't speak to me hardly at all. My mother says Dad's disappointed with me, but it's been a long time. Alejandra Martinez, pregnant at fourteen.

Many pregnant teenagers live with single mothers. They are likely to have a tough time dealing with the changes brought about by the baby. However, those young women who live with

both parents sometimes face added emotional stress—along with
added support. A teen's relationship with her father can be very
special. If that relationship remains special throughout her pregnancy and through the months and years ahead, everyone wins.

Father Hurt by Daughter's Pregnancy

If a father has had a close relationship with his daughter, he
may be even more upset by her pregnancy. Perhaps the obvious
fact that she has been sexually active is disturbing to him. This
is his little girl who one day would grow up and marry, but not
now, not yet.

Watching his daughter change as her body becomes fuller
and the pregnancy more and more obvious is disturbing to
someone who perhaps, until now, considered pregnancy a
private phenomenon between himself and his wife. His daughter's changing body is a constant reminder that she has been
sexually active and, even more relevant, not only his daughter,
but he and his wife are facing drastic changes in their lives.

Alejandra was Alicia and Joe Martinez's only daughter. Her
pregnancy at fourteen was a shock, especially because Alicia
and Joe intensely disliked Alejandra's boyfriend, Sal. Alicia
explained, "You have to remember Alejandra was still a child,
and it was hard for Joe to understand that she was involved with
sex. And you can't treat her like a child when she has a child of
her own."

Whatever the reason, Alejandra's relationship with her father
is causing her great sadness. She appears to crave his approval
and support as she says, "Dad don't speak to me hardly at all.
My mother says Dad's disappointed with me, but it's been a
long time. Eric and I lived with Mom and Dad until Eric was
three. Dad and I were fairly close before all of this because I was
into sports, and you know how fathers like sports.

"I still cry to this day. I wish me and my father were close.
When I see Eric and him give each other kisses and hugs, it
makes me smile. It also hurts a lot."

Alejandra's mother tried to explain, "Even today Joe never
sits down and talks to Alejandra. She says, 'He doesn't like me.'
What do you say then?

"I tell my husband, and he laughs and says, 'She gets on my nerves. Let her suffer.' I know it hurt him a lot when she ran away, but I wish they could be close again."

"Men Don't Cry"

Many men have been reared with the "Men don't cry" syndrome. They find it difficult to show their feelings or to share those feelings, even with someone close.

While Dad is going through his own trauma, his daughter needs his support now more than ever. Giving her the cold shoulder, accusing her of being a slut, or other thoughtless actions won't help.

Jerry Hertzel remembers asking his daughter, Maggie, "What were you thinking about? Don't you know anything about birth control?"

"I didn't think it would happen to me," she said. According to her father, she was going through a wild period in her life before she got pregnant, and it caught up with her.

"I had trouble accepting Maggie's pregnancy. I couldn't talk to anybody about it," Jerry related. "I didn't even tell anybody at work until after she delivered. I was ashamed of her at the time, I really was. I did tell my boss about it. I said, 'If I have my ups and downs, that's probably why.' It was hard for me. I felt betrayed."

If a couple is having marital problems, their teenage daughter's pregnancy may appear to be the straw that breaks their marriage. This happened to Delores and Guy Hamlin. Guy left soon after they learned of Belinda's pregnancy. He and Delores no longer could afford their house, so Delores and Belinda moved into an apartment. "We'd been having problems, but I thought we had started to work them out," Delores said. "I guess we hadn't."

Guy Hamlin had an extremely difficult time with his daughter's pregnancy. Delores recalls, "When Guy found out Belinda was pregnant, he was ready to take her in for an abortion immediately. They yelled at each other for days, and finally he went to see a psychiatrist. The psychiatrist told him, 'You've got to do what's best for your child.' Guy calmed down after

that, but Belinda and I moved out when she was about seven
months pregnant."

Frank Hernandez related, "One thing I won't do, I'll never
mention the pregnancy. It's just like you get a person down and
the last thing you want to do is remind them of it. I've never to
this day told Blanca, 'Look what you've done, look at what
happened to you.' I don't think there's anything to be gained by
doing that."

Warren Boltz remembers facing his daughter's pregnancy
announcement. "My first feeling was devastation," he said. "I
was truly shaken by it. I was upset that this could happen to
Lupe, and that she let it happen. I had no idea she was involved
in this kind of a relationship. It was all news to me.

> *"I knew we had to get with it,*
> *find the medical care, the counseling,*
> *planning for the baby."*

"Lupe didn't take it lightly either. It was obvious we all had
to go through this together. It would be easier if we stayed
together and cooperated. Actually, I got over the devastation
pretty quickly because I knew we had to get with it, find the
medical care, the counseling, planning for the baby."

Sometimes a father, in spite of (or because of) the intense
pain he's feeling, manages to take a leadership role in helping
his wife and his daughter cope with the stresses caused by the
pregnancy. Jessica Williams appreciated Lee's assistance in
this area.

She commented, "Lee was the biggest help I had. Without his
calm support, I would have lost it time and again. Arlana and I
would get into it a lot, and he would always find the right words
to say to each of us.

"I don't know how a single parent or someone whose husband is not supportive survives. I can also see how we could
have split up. We disagreed on a number of things, but we
worked them out. You can get to your wit's end about so many
other issues that you forget about your own relationship. We had
to guard against letting this mess that up."

Communication Is Critical

Many fathers have little time to devote to their families. He may be extremely busy earning a living. He may be involved in church and community activities. Or he may hide in front of the TV screen. Whatever the reason, he may have difficulty making time to talk through the decisions and the changes facing his daughter, her mother, himself, and the rest of his family.

Jerry Hertzel stressed the importance of communication: "You've got to talk about things that are bothering you. I remember as a kid when I did something wrong, I was punished. At first I felt my daughter should be punished, but that's not something she needs from us. She *is* being punished because her life has changed.

"We were up front about our willingness to be grandparents and to babysit one night a week. But our lives are going on. We said, 'If you're going to bring your baby into our house, you'll live by our rules.' Her life has changed. Ours has, too, but not as much as I thought it would."

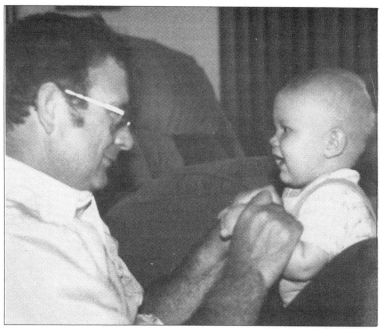

"We babysit one night a week."

When Blanca Hernandez, sixteen, told her parents, Frank and
Lorraine, that she was pregnant, her father was especially upset.
Frank told Blanca she must get Edwardo, the baby's father, over
immediately to talk about their plans.

When Edwardo arrived, Frank did most of the talking. He
told Edwardo he didn't have to marry Blanca, that her parents
would take care of her, but Edwardo said he wanted to marry
her. Blanca agreed that this would be best although her parents
pointed out how young they were and some of the trials they
would be facing. Frank said, "We talked with Blanca for three
days. We told her this was a big step, and that she didn't have to
marry Edwardo."

Blanca and Edwardo were married, but the agreement was
that they would live with Blanca's parents. Edwardo would have
preferred to live with his parents, but he moved in with Blanca
for awhile.

"Blanca realized pretty quick how insecure Edwardo was,"
Frank continued. "He was twenty, but he wanted to go back to
live with his mother. We let them go there to live on alternate
months. Finally Blanca told us Edwardo wasn't ready to leave
home. He couldn't hold a job for more than a month, and that
upset us. At the end of that year, they were divorced.

---

*"It's important not to feel you've let your kids down.
Don't think of yourselves as parents who failed."*

"Like most parents, we always hoped this (daughter's pregnancy) wouldn't happen to us. Like other parents, we were in
shock at first. You say, 'What happened here? What did I do
wrong? Were we too strict? Not strict enough?' You have to
step lightly because you don't want your daughter to rebel now.

"It's important not to feel you've let your kids down. You
can't dwell in the past. Don't think of yourself as parents who
failed. You always ask yourself, 'Why us?' and you don't get
an answer."

Frank shared some advice a friend had given him. "One day,
not long after we learned Blanca was pregnant, a friend must
have read it in my face because he asked me what was wrong.

"I started telling him what was going on, and he said, 'Frank, you know what? I had the same thing happen to me when my daughter was fifteen. Look, life is hard—you always think these things happen only to other people. But what makes you think you're so special that it can't happen to you? You're nobody special. Things happen, and the important thing is how you adjust to it, how you make the best of it.'"

Toby Erickson's Story

Toby Erickson talked about many issues concerning his fifteen-year-old daughter Jamie's pregnancy. Jamie's daughter, Dori, was born two months ago.

When my wife (Monica) told me Jamie was pregnant, I went into shock. I felt like I held my breath for thirty minutes, like if I breathed, I was going to explode. I felt betrayed as a father, and I felt a great loss for Jamie because at fifteen she was no way ready to be a parent, yet there it was. After her mother told me, I let it soak in for nearly an hour. Then I finally talked to Jamie.

The first thing I said was, "It's a hell of a way to lose your childhood."

Here's my fifteen-year-old daughter, and you're telling me she's going to be a mother, and she's still a little girl. At fifteen, a sophomore in high school, just starting to realize what the world is all about, and it's a shock.

She wasn't ready to be a mother, but thanks to her school and to the counseling she got at Catholic Social Services, she got the help she needed. The counselor talked to Monica and me a couple of times, too. I don't know what we would have done without her. The Teen Parent Program helped tremendously.

Our church was supportive to a point. We're surprised that there isn't a place for Monica and me to get support in our local parish. Our friends have supported us, but counseling wasn't available there. We had to go through the Archdiocese.

I felt like I was in limbo those first two or three months. This was a major change in our life style. Financially, it was a big change because it will be awhile before she can go out on her own—probably a couple of years longer because she has the baby. We had talked about early retirement, about not waiting until I was sixty-five, but the added financial responsibility of the baby means that's gone by the wayside.

At first I worried a lot about the financial part. Finally I realized it wasn't all that important. It's not a big deal. Jamie is more important to me than that. The early retirement thing wasn't that important.

Of course we talked about whether she wanted to keep the baby. That was her decision, but one of the things I told her was that she was going to finish her education. That's a must.

This has been a major change for our whole family. However, it's been a good—well, not a good situation, but a growing situation. It's made the three of us more aware of each other as people because of the things we've gone through.

The support of Jamie's brothers and sisters has surprised me. They were all behind her one hundred percent when they learned she wanted to keep the baby. That was a positive to me.

The day Dori was born I was scared to death. I was in the delivery room with her, and I kept thinking, "The baby is going to be here," and I felt fear for Jamie. Would she be able to accept the responsibility, the heavy load that was being placed on her shoulders? Most of my concerns were for her, and not so much for myself. I can make the changes in my life that are needed for her and the baby because she is my daughter and I love her very much. My family means a lot to me so the transition has been easier than I thought it would be.

> "Dori is a special joy to us now,
> a very bright part of our lives."

Dori is a special joy to us now, a very bright part of our lives. She's a happy little person. She hardly ever fusses. The only problem is, Monica and I don't have the free time we'd have if she weren't here.

The school has a childcare center, so we knew Jamie could continue there, but she also needed to get a job. Before Dori was born, we told Jamie we would not be surrogate parents, but we would be available to babysit while she worked.

We had agreed, however, that Jamie would have to make arrangements for Dorie's care when we had other plans. So far, that has worked. She has accepted the responsibility. There haven't been major crises—yet. There was a lot of tentativeness when they first came home—how are we going to handle this? What's going to happen when something comes up? So far, we realize we worked ourselves into a worry over something that hasn't happened.

"That nine months changed our lives completely."

It is not wonderful, but we are making it work. I love the baby, but I still think my daughter would be better off if she didn't have her. As much as we love Dori, this has changed Jamie's whole life. We don't see her old friends any more. There's still a stigma attached to having a baby when you're in high school. I don't think it's so much her friends as it is their parents. I run into them occasionally, and they say, "Well, we'll have to stop to see the baby." But they don't talk about the person, they talk about the "thing."

That nine months changed our lives completely. Jamie isn't at all the same person she was. I don't think any of us are. It changes your whole outlook on what is important and what is not, and some of it is hard to face. Part of the change may be harder on the parents than it is on the daughter. Acceptance of the reality may be hardest on the father. I'm very protective of my daughters, and this was not supposed to happen. I'm protective, and I'm proud. I'm still proud of Jamie. She made a mistake, she has to live with it, and she's doing a good job of handling it. But it's a shame that a young girl can make this mistake and have to pay for it the rest of her life.

Advice for other fathers? At first, you have to hold your counsel to yourself while you let what's happening soak in. Don't over-react to a situation you can't control. You don't have control over this, and you have to accept what's happening.

I'd say to fathers, "Don't be afraid to let your wife and daughter know you need support, too, you need help, too." I was

protective of my feelings until I talked to Maureen (counselor).
If you lash out too soon, you can cause too much hurt.
    It was a hard time, and if I hadn't eventually opened up, I
think I would have had a real problem. Men aren't supposed to
cry. I have worked in youth programs, and that's helped me let
my feelings show a little more. We've got to be willing to sit
down and say, "I'm really hurting, and I need to talk to some-
body about this." I have seen people so hurt they won't talk to
anybody. They feel betrayed.

Paying the Bills

While a pregnant teenager's father must deal with his emotions, he also faces the financial realities of adding another baby
to his household. In most of the families interviewed for this
book, the baby's father offered little financial support. Some of
the young mothers worked to support their babies, but if they
did, they needed babysitters. Working even part-time is difficult
for a teen mother who is also attending school and taking the
primary responsibility for her child.

Don Gray was the breadwinner in his family, and was antici-
pating early retirement. Robin's pregnancy when she was
sixteen changed all that. Don said, "I'm almost sixty, and Lois
and I haven't had any time together. Robin's pregnancy made
me feel we aren't ever going to travel. We aren't going to do all
those things we had planned. This took away all thoughts of
early retirement.

"My biggest fear was the financial part. I didn't know what to
expect. My insurance paid for the birth, but the baby wasn't
covered. After Roni was born, however, Robin applied again to
social services, and they issued a medical card for Roni. That's a
big help—Roni's been in the hospital twice and to the doctor
about every other week since she was born five months ago.

"The money part of it still is my biggest worry."

She Wants Her Dad in Delivery

Several fathers of students in our Teen Mother Program
coached their daughters through labor and delivery. Curtis
Fletcher didn't coach his daughter, but Carole asked for her

father when she learned she would have a Cesarean delivery. Curtis got to the hospital minutes before Carole went to the operating room. Her mother commented, "When Carole's dad came in, he kissed her and said, 'Everything will be OK,' and she was off to the operating room. The baby's father, his mother, and I were all there, but Carole wanted her daddy."

Jerry Hertzel was also with his daughter, Maggie, when she gave birth. Maggie's mother, Sylvia, was her labor coach, but Jerry joined them at the hospital. Sylvia related, "The nurse asked him if he wanted to stay. He monitored every labor contraction, and when she was giving birth, he was right there, cradling her head and telling her to push. When she gave birth, the doctor was crying, the nurse was crying, I think we all were.

"Neither of us touched Tyson until he and Maggie had a chance to bond. I felt this was important because I didn't want any mix-up as to who his mother was. After that, Jerry held Tyson, and then the four of us held each other. It was a very special time. From that moment on, Jerry has adored Tyson."

Grandfather-to-Be Shares His Feelings

Cyndi Green made an adoption plan. She didn't intend to see her baby, but in the hospital, she and Brad held, fed, and loved Kristin before they released her to foster care. Three days later Cyndi, with Brad's approval, decided to parent Kristin.

Palmer Green, Cyndi's father, shared his feelings about his daughter's pregnancy, his reaction to her adoption/keeping dilemma, and some tips for other fathers facing similar situations. He also reveals his strategy for dealing with feelings he can't talk about:

My first thought was, "Oh shit, how is her mom going to react to this? How is Cyndi going to be?" We were in good enough shape financially so it was mostly the emotional things. Then I figured, well, it's too late to holler, and that wouldn't do any good anyway. When I was a kid, I didn't listen either.

I told them I wasn't going to be tough about it. I never beat her yet, and I see no sense in starting now. I suppose I'm a realist. But now what?

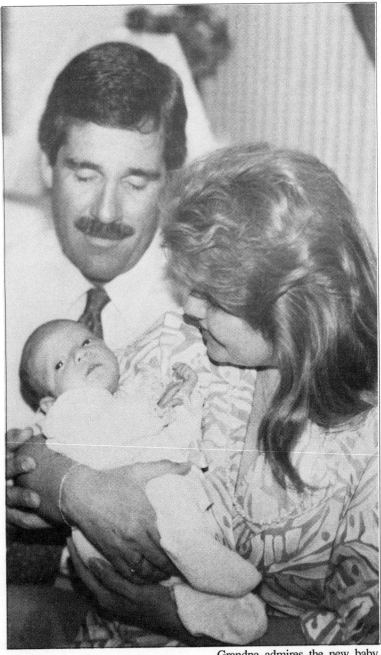

Grandpa admires the new baby.

*"You've got some big decisions to make," I told her. "Now
it's real, now you aren't a kid no more." I told her she had three
options and she had better think about each one, the good and
the bad, not only for today, but tomorrow, next month, and the
years ahead. Each one has its pros and cons, and she'd better be
sure. We'd try to help her, but she'd have to think hard about it
and make her decision.*

*At that point I wasn't real impressed with Brad (baby's
father). I didn't want to take him out to dinner. But past experience told me it takes two to tango. It happened to me when I was
a kid, and they don't need somebody chewing their ass. Hell,
they already know that. I tried to be neutral with them.*

"My feelings get hurt real easy,
and most of my life I've tried to hide that."

---

*I hadn't made up my mind yet. Too many times kids will say
one thing and do another. I said to myself, we'll wait and see.
Two months, six months after she's born, we'll know more about
what's going on.*

*My feelings get hurt real easy, and most of my life I've tried
to hide that. When Kristin came along I purposefully kept myself
distant . . . it's like bringing a kid a new puppy and then later
taking it away, and I didn't want to go through that hurt. I didn't
want to get attached if she wasn't going to be there. It wouldn't
do me any good, and it wouldn't do her any good. And I didn't
want it to cloud my judgment. It was easier for me to remain
distant from Kristin so I wouldn't influence Cyndi, and so my
feelings didn't get hurt.*

*I did this until I felt pretty sure Kristin was going to hang
around—probably a couple of months. It takes time. Then when
there was no more talk about adoption, I let it set for awhile. I
didn't hear anything, and everything seemed to be going pretty
good. I thought, well now, I can start taking an interest.*

*Before we jump on somebody else, we need to put ourselves
in the other person's shoes. What would help you and what
would hurt you? Swap places. That helps me because most of the
time I've been there. Hollering and screaming don't do any*

good at a time like this when everybody is scared anyway. She
needs your trust and support.

Kids should talk to their parents, and parents should listen to
what kids say. If the parent doesn't listen to the kid, whose fault
is it? Kids aren't soldiers, they are young people, and they need
to learn. You can help them by telling them what you know—
"This won't work because . . ." "You need to go to school."

Don't worry your kids, talk to them, give them examples of
the right way and the wrong way, and let them decide. You'll be
surprised how they can figure it out.

Don't throw money at them. They don't need that. We all
need money, but it's not the cure. They need your time and your
understanding. And put yourselves in their boots. If the same
thing had happened to you at that age, what could your parents
have told you that would have helped?

We're taking some responsibility for Kristin, but Cyndi and
Brad are doing all right, actually pretty good. Of course they
don't know everything, but they could be doing a lot worse—and
I suppose they could be doing better. Actually, they have a lot
going for them.

One of the things Cyndi and Brad have going for them is their
parents' love and support. Sometimes emotional support from
their parents is even more important to young people than is
financial help. Many teenage parents need both.

CHAPTER 4

Is Baby's Father Involved?

*I was scared at first, confused about what we were going to
do. Now we both take care of her as well as we can without
living in the same house. I think it's important for a child to
know both parents are there for her.* Brad, father at seventeen.

*Abby felt Tom had certain rights while I thought he had none
because he hadn't shown any love, care, protection, or assistance at any time. Now Abby agrees with me.* Katheryn Peters,
mother of Abby, pregnant at fifteen.

*Peter's father is not involved. It's a little hard to handle
because my son, as he grows up, will know his father lives down
the street, and he doesn't even want to see Peter.* Lupe Boltz,
mother of one-year-old Peter.

*As I look back, I don't think anybody tuned in to his needs. It
was just "What will you do?" and not "What are you feeling?"
I don't think we thought he needed anything.* Kathleen Jacobs,
mother of Lance, father at seventeen.

What about the father of the baby? The stereotype of teenage
fathers is the young man who runs, who doesn't care about his
baby or the baby's mother, probably denies paternity, and will
never contribute to his child's financial support. Part of that
stereotype is the idea that most fathers of babies born to teenage
mothers are teenagers themselves.

However, only twenty-eight percent of the babies born to
teenage mothers in California in 1986 were fathered by men
who were teenagers themselves, according to a survey reported
in *Adolescent Pregnancy and Parenting in California* by Brindis
and Jeremy (1988: University of California, San Francisco).
Almost three in four men who father babies born to teenage
women are twenty years old or older.

Legal Rights and Responsibilities

If the child's parents do not marry, what is the father's
responsibility? Laws vary from state to state, but generally the
father and the mother have equal parental rights and equal
responsibilities.

Whether or not the man named is actually the father of the
child can now be determined with one hundred percent accuracy
through DNA testing, according to attorney Lawrence Treglia,
Huntington Beach, California. From a legal standpoint, the
crucial concern is the rights of the child, he points out.

"The court looks at the parent as being the protector and
guardian of the rights of the child, and the laws are set up to
make sure that child has the best possible chance," Treglia
explained.

Treglia recommends putting the father's name on the birth
certificate because this makes it easier to identify him as the
father in the future. For example, the child may become eligible
for Social Security benefits from his father, and it seems unfair
to the child to make them more difficult to obtain, Treglia said.
However, Social Security benefits can be awarded to a child
even if his father's name is not on the child's birth certificate.

Some young mothers tell me they want nothing to do with
their child's father. To this, Treglia responds, "Can the mother
really support the child on her own? If she can't, she may be

depriving the child of some economic status or perhaps health care insurance the child is entitled to. For example, if the father becomes wealthy, he could be court-ordered to pay a substantial part of his income to that child. Does the mother have the right to deprive the child of that possible benefit in the future?"

Maggie Hertzel assumes that because she didn't put her baby's father's name on the birth certificate, he has no rights. She commented, "I've made out a will that says if anything were to happen to me, he'd not be contacted. When medical records ask for the father's name, I put N/A."

Treglia, however, asserts that by law one cannot control another's actions. If the father in this case decided to come forward and assert his rights and responsibilities to the child, the courts would probably approve.

The Adams family met once with Marisa's father and his family, but neither Dick nor his parents provided any support. A year after Marisa was born, Colette went to court to prove Dick was the father of her child. She felt that Marisa needed to know her father's identity. After that, Dick agreed to release his rights to Marisa in return for his release from all financial support requirements.

Laws vary from state to state, but it's doubtful an agreement such as this would be upheld by the court if any interested party should ask that it be set aside, according to Treglia. "A parent cannot make a legal contract to abrogate (annul) his duty to support that child," he explained.

It is important to remember that laws vary from state to state in the United States and from province to province in Canada. For information concerning a father's rights and responsibilities, contact an attorney in your area who specializes in family law.

Some Marry Before Delivery

Across the United States, about thirty-nine percent of teenage mothers marry the father of their baby before delivery. Of the twenty-eight families interviewed for this book, only two of the young couples married before their child was born, and five were married later. Two couples were married only a short time, then divorced.

The three couples who were married one to two years after childbirth all appear to be doing well several years later. However, one of these couples was not together at all during the wife's pregnancy, another had difficulties in their relationship during the pregnancy, and the third couple recently split up for a few months but is now back together.

Six (twenty-one percent) of the babies' fathers in this study (including one who married the baby's mother) had major problems including drug involvement and partner abuse. Ten fathers (thirty-six percent) were not involved with their babies' mothers significantly throughout pregnancy or after delivery, and two others split not long after delivery. In addition to the five married couples, four other couples are still together.

Sometimes Marriage Works

The couple with the best track record among these families is the Todds—the best track record because Phil and Angie's marriage is now six years old, and the couple agrees they have a good relationship.

Their oldest daughter, Rachel, is now eight, and they have two little boys aged two and four. Phil completed college two years ago and now has a good job. Angie finished two years of college and works part-time. Their life together is good, but their relationship suffered during Angie's first pregnancy.

Phil was seventeen and still in high school when Angie, a college freshman, conceived. Angie and her mother were not happy about the situation, but they checked out Angie's options, and during pregnancy, Angie was making an adoption plan.

Phil was embarrassed as Angie grew larger. He didn't want his friends to know, at least not until after graduation from the all-boys school he attended. Yet Angie would be seven months pregnant at graduation. Angie recalled, "He'd come over and see me, but things were not the same. He was kind of cold, very scared. At least he stayed with me.

"I didn't show until I was six months pregnant. I bought a dress that hid any signs of pregnancy because I wanted to go to Phil's senior prom. He ended up taking somebody else, and that hurt. Looking back, he feels real crummy about that.

"Phil said he'd go to Lamaze classes with me, but the first night he didn't show up. He said he was too embarrassed. From then on, though, he went with me, and he was a big help during labor and delivery.

"If we saw each other, it was at my mom's house. We didn't go out. The adoption counselor told him I needed to go out with him, whether to a movie or dinner in the city where nobody would know us. Now Phil tells me it was hard for him to see me looking more and more pregnant because he felt so guilty about it all.

"I decided to keep Rachel, and Phil was very supportive. He was away at college part of the time, but our relationship improved steadily. We were married a week after Rachel's second birthday. We had a week's honeymoon with my mom taking care of Rachel half the time and his mom the other half. Then we went away to school, and everything has turned out well for us."

Couple's Adoption Plan Changes

Cyndi Green and Brad Wilson appear to mirror somewhat the early part of the Todds' relationship. Their daughter, Kristin, is six months old.

Cyndi, sixteen, and Brad, seventeen, had been dating for three years when Cyndi became pregnant. They were both scared and didn't know what to do. Their relationship had been going downhill, "real rocky," according to Cyndi.

Cyndi's mother, Jackie, recalled, "At first they wanted to get married and raise the baby together. But the pressure was too much for both of them. Brad changed his mind . . . he seemed real flighty at that time, probably felt like he was backed into a corner. They were both running scared—kids taking on adult responsibilities.

"Cyndi wanted to get away from here, from her friends and her school, so we sent her to Minnesota to be with my brother. Then we discovered Brad was going too. We were disappointed because we wanted them to have this time apart. Cyndi stayed with my brother while Brad got an apartment and found a job.

"They continued arguing, however, and Brad was back home within a month.

"Four weeks before Kristin was born, Cyndi came home. She was planning to place the baby for adoption, and she and Brad stayed away from each other until Kristin was born.

"Brad rushed to the hospital to see the baby, and he held her in the nursery. So did I, and so did his mother. We took turns.

"Cyndi had said she didn't want to see the baby before it was placed. However, the day after Kristin was born, Cyndi decided to spend some time with her. She and Brad were with her for several hours, then placed her in foster care for three days."

Cyndi continued the story: "The first time Brad saw Kristin, he wanted to keep her, but he didn't pressure me, and neither did my parents. It was my decision.

"I was miserable those three days she was in foster care. I didn't feel right about it at all, so we picked Kristin up and brought her home. We had nothing in the house for the baby, but my family and Brad's family rushed around finding the things we needed.

"Brad was real happy. We spend most of our time together now when he's not working and I'm not in school."

Brad described his feelings after his daughter was born. "That was pretty sad. I wanted to keep her, but I didn't think we could do it. I held her a lot at the hospital, and I was feeling pretty bad. Cyndi and I talked, and we decided to go through with the adoption. Three days later she called me at work and told me she wanted to keep Kristin. I was pleased.

"I felt uncomfortable with the whole situation that first month or two. It took me a little while to get adjusted, but now I'm here every day. We take care of Kristin together although I don't live with Cyndi and her parents. I take Kristin some nights, and I watch her all day on the weekends. We both take care of her as well as we can without living in the same house. I think it's important for a child to know both parents are there for her."

Brad and Cyndi set their wedding date for four months after Kristin's birth, then called it off. They decided not to rush into marriage, although they plan to marry eventually.

Cyndi will graduate from high school in the spring, and a week after Kristin's first birthday, she and Brad will enroll at a college seventy-five miles from their homes. They will take Kristin and move into campus family housing. The college provides limited daycare. Brad's sister will also be there with her child, and the two families plan to share babysitting and to schedule their classes around their children's care.

Palmer Green, Cyndi's father, succinctly observed, "When they go to college next year, they'll get another taste of reality. When you have a little one, it changes the rules of the game a whole bunch. It's all right if you don't eat for a day or two, but when that little one doesn't eat, that's no good. But I think they're going to make it."

Parents Disapprove But Relationship Continues

Three couples in these families are continuing to some extent their relationship although, in each case, the young woman's parents have their doubts about the wisdom of this approach.

The Fletchers don't like Darin much. He's been in trouble with the police, mostly speeding tickets. His relationship with Carole has been off and on. Irene Fletcher said, "They broke up for a couple of months and Carole dated another guy, but now she's back with him. He's nineteen and he's working, although he quit his job for several months last year to play football his senior year of high school. He doesn't take much responsibility, and you can't shove it down his throat. He's not the person we want Carole to marry, but what can we say? If that's who she chooses, that's her decision.

"Darin has a lot of good qualities, but he had no parental supervision when he was growing up.

"We tried not letting Carole see Darin but found that didn't work. We'd tell her she couldn't see him, then find she was sneaking and lying and seeing him anyway, then she would be punished and he'd get off scot-free.

"We went to family counseling for awhile. The counselor told us that, with Carole and Darin already bonded to each other through sex and having a baby together, we probably couldn't keep them from seeing each other. Kelli is our grandchild, and we need to remember that fifty percent of her comes from Darin.

"We figure the less we say about Darin, the better off we are. Now Carole's back with him. When he comes to our house, he has to respect our wishes, and we don't see much of him."

Carole lets Kelli spend the night with her father occasionally. She reported, "My parents were strongly against having Kelli spend the night at her father's house. They didn't think she should even go over there without me because my mother thought they wouldn't take good care of her. But I told them this was the only way her father could accept the fact that he has a daughter, and he has to do that if he's going to be responsible for Kelli.

"The first time Darin watched Kelli overnight was when we were broken up and I went out with someone else. Darin did quite well with Kelli. I knew he would—I have a lot of faith in him, but my parents don't, and that's where we disagree. I wish they could learn to like him."

His Mother Babysits

Juana Wolfe's parents, Estella and Kevin, were disappointed when Juana, nineteen, dropped out of college because of her pregnancy. Estella related, "We didn't like the baby's father, hoped she'd meet somebody better, get away from people she was with. Unfortunately, it didn't work out that way. Greg never graduated from high school, never got his GED (General Educational Development), and has never held a job for more than two months.

"Greg's mother takes care of the baby while Juana works. I don't like that situation, but what can I say unless I quit my job and babysit?

"I try not to be negative about Greg, but Juana knows exactly how we feel. He started a new job two weeks ago, but he doesn't like it. Juana tells him, 'Too bad, you have to work.'

"Greg's mother talked to me about grandparent rights, so I checked with an attorney and learned we have no grandparent rights in this state." (The law dealing with this issue varies from state to state, but in California, if a grandparent wants to go to court to assert visitation rights, their request may be granted, according to attorney Lawrence Treglia. This may be possible even if their son/daughter does not have custody of the child.)

Juana added, "I'm on a friendly basis with Greg, although he's not working now and that's hard. I don't know whether

I want to go for child support. I think he should want to help us. When he's working, if I need something, he'll get it for me.

"Greg just turned twenty-one, but he's kind of . . . his mom did everything for him, and he has never had to work. She still helps him too much. It's getting tough because I pay all the bills myself, and I get angry. Ricki is with Greg during the day because his mother takes care of him when I'm working."

Some young mothers say they don't want to insist on child support from their baby's father. However, it's usually best if the father, like Greg, is not providing regular financial support, to apply through the courts for that support. Otherwise, the child is the one who is likely to be cheated if his father doesn't provide for him.

If It's Your Son

Juana's older brother fathered a child three years ago, and he and his baby's mother were married a year later. The Wolfes talked about that situation, and the difference in their feelings when their son caused an early pregnancy versus their daughter being pregnant:

Kevin: "We expected Al to carry his load. Even before they were married, he did so. He was in love with Connie, and we always thought they'd get married. She was seventeen, he was twenty-one when Sonya was born."

Estella: "Connie is the nicest person. I was devastated then, too, because she had started college and had to come home because she was pregnant. We knew she wanted to go to school, and I was upset because this would change her entire life."

Kevin: "We were especially concerned because Al, although he was twenty-one, didn't seem real mature to us. But it's worked out fine. He's in the Navy now."

Estella: "Connie's mother wanted them to get married immediately although she didn't much like Al at the time, and I understand that. She was going through a lot more than I was. I thought getting married would be two mistakes instead of one."

Kevin: "In a teenage pregnancy, it's more difficult to be the father of the girl than to be the father of the boy. Juana's pregnancy was much more traumatic for me."

Baby's Father Is Immature

Two young mothers contributing to this book had fairly
positive relationships with their partners for a short time, then
split. Keegan Colby, barely sixteen, and Robin, a few months
older, were close throughout pregnancy. Keegan's parents were
supportive.

Don, Robin's father, commented approvingly, "Keegan and
his family's support helped Robin a lot. So often the boy denies
it, and I think he was a great crutch for her."

Keegan was with Robin through labor and delivery, and so
was his mother. "I really liked the kid until right before the baby
was born, and then I started feeling these vibes," she said.

Lois describes Keegan's mother as domineering, and Keegan
as "a big baby." "He takes no responsibility at all, and I have a
hard time tolerating that, although I know it's not his fault."

The first week after Robin and Roni came home from the
hospital, Keegan spent many hours in the Gray home. However,
according to Lois, "Keegan got all pouty because he thought
Robin wasn't giving him enough attention." Lois was also
exasperated with Keegan's parents who were "going to do this
and going to do that, but never sent anything, not one can of
formula, nothing. It went from bad to worse."

During the months that followed, Keegan showed the basic
immaturity typical of a sixteen-year-old. He promised to pay
half the daycare fee required so Robin could return to school,
but "It was like pulling teeth to get it," Lois reported.

Finally Robin had had enough. "I get up every day. I go to
school. I work. I'm up with the baby at night, and you don't do
anything. Your mother even pays for daycare, not you," Robin
told him. As a result, they have broken up, and Robin wants
nothing more to do with Keegan.

Lois sees much of the problem belonging to Keegan's mother.
"Keegan is not growing up at all, and Robin is. He isn't accepting responsibility, and Robin is. His mother isn't helping him
until she says, 'Look, this is your baby. You work, and you give
the money to Robin.' Until this happens, he won't even try.

"Robin has talked to a lawyer about what she can and can't
do. She doesn't want Keegan to have anything to do with Roni,

but he says he's going to get visitation rights. I don't know what would be right.

"This has been hard on Robin because she said for such a long time that she loved him. It's hard on her trying to deal with the baby and deal with him. I feel she has tried hard to be responsible, and he isn't trying at all. He'd walk out of the room when she changed Roni's diaper because 'It made him sick.'

"I honestly think the baby and everyone else would be just as well off without Keegan in the picture. If he gets visitation rights, he won't be the one taking care of the baby. His mother will. The Saturday they came home from the hospital, she was holding Roni. Keegan wanted to hold her, and his mother said, 'Oh, you can't hold her until you sit down. Now sit down, and I'll give you the baby. Be real careful now.'"

Robin's analysis of Keegan is much briefer: "He's a jerk. He couldn't face the fact that Roni comes first. He didn't like that so he got fed up and left. I'm glad he's gone."

Keegan Colby's biggest fault
is being only sixteen and the son of a mother
who hasn't helped him grow up.

Apparently Keegan Colby's biggest fault is being only sixteen and the son of a mother who hasn't helped him grow up. If Robin's pregnancy had happened several years later, the young couple might have coped well together. But Robin was sixteen, and Keegan several months younger, two very normal high school kids not yet ready for the adult world of parenthood.

As often happens with pregnant teenagers, Robin matured a lot during her pregnancy. Her parents expected her to take responsibility for her baby, stay in school, and get a job to help with the baby's expenses. Robin managed to handle her triple roles while Keegan neither worked nor cared for the baby.

In fairness to Keegan, he didn't get a lot of help during this stressful period. His mother considered him her little boy, not ready to take on the responsibilities of fatherhood. He and his mother would have been welcome at the teen father and grandparent support groups at Robin's school, but neither attended.

Father Not Involved

Ten (thirty-six percent) of the fathers of the babies in this survey did not continue their relationship with the young mother after they learned of her pregnancy. For example, Stacy's boyfriend "kind of disappeared" while Stacy was pregnant. "Kenny visited once when Patrice was four months old," Stacy remembered. "His mother wanted to see Patrice several times, but once I met my husband, she faded away, too. She goes to our church, but I think she doesn't want to intrude. She speaks to us, and once she asked me for a family picture.

"My husband adopted Patrice, and his parents are Patrice's grandparents. When I met Arlo, he accepted Patrice as his own. If it was hard for him, he never let me know. Patrice knows she's adopted, but if someone were to tell her Arlo's parents are not her grandparents, she'd say, 'Oh, yes, they are.'

"For the adoption process, the papers were mailed to Kenny, and he signed them all, then mailed them back."

A good resource to offer a child who has never known his father is *Do I Have a Daddy? A Story About a Single-Parent Child* (Morning Glory Press). It's a picture story for the child, and it includes a ten-page section of suggestions for single mothers who must deal with this question.

Tragedy of Physical Abuse

Other relationships were not so benign. Fathers of the babies of one in five of the young women interviewed had severe problems. At least three young mothers were physically abused by their partners, and this group included one young couple married for three months.

Beth Ann Hanley, seventeen, and Lyle James, twenty-one, had dated a year when Beth Ann conceived. During her pregnancy, according to Beth Ann's mother, Peggy, Lyle seemed attentive and caring. He wanted to marry Beth Ann immediately, but Peggy and Adrian insisted that she finish her four remaining months of high school first.

Lyle's personality seemed to change as soon as Yvette was born. He became extremely possessive. He and Beth Ann started fighting, and Beth Ann thought she could make it better by getting married. Their wedding was six weeks later. They moved about three miles from Beth Ann's parents.

They were married three months. "They'd been married about four weeks when Beth Ann came to me and told me how unhappy she was," Peggy explained. "I chalked it up to a new marriage until she started telling me what was happening—the fits of anger, the physical abuse. I suggested she see a counselor which she did. The counselor told her she had to get away from Lyle because she was putting not only herself in jeopardy, but also Yvette.

"Adrian, our sons, and I went over one afternoon and helped Beth Ann move out and back home. Adrian called Lyle at work and told him they should talk before he went home. They did."

Beth Ann added, "After three months, it was a clean break on my side, but Lyle continued to harass me and to fight the divorce. He takes Yvette every other weekend, but we make the transition from the daycare center so I don't see him."

Beth Ann's father, Adrian, commented, "One of the problems in being pregnant and planning a wedding is the focus is then on the baby and the pregnancy. The focus is not on the marriage. The time you would have spent getting to know each other and deciding if this is the individual you want to marry is over-shadowed by the pregnancy and by the baby. It makes it difficult for young people to sort these things out, to determine who they are and what they really want to do.

"The emotional turmoil of an unwanted pregnancy for a teenager in high school, the emotion within the family—all these things take away from the focus of the marriage. We wanted Beth Ann and Lyle to delay the wedding for awhile longer. We didn't want them to get married because of the baby, but that was not to be."

What's a Parent to Do?

The odds are not great for the success of a relationship started during early adolescence and faced with the stress of too-early pregnancy and parenthood. In this sample, only nine (thirty-two percent) of the couples are still together. Both the teen mothers' parents and the teens themselves described rather serious

problems within nearly half of the relationships of these
still-together couples.

What "should" a young couple do? How much "should" her
parents (and his) get involved? Do the rest of us have any
responsibility for providing services to help young couples
prepare to live independently?

The answer, of course, varies from family to family. If your
daughter is being physically abused by her partner, by all means
encourage, do whatever you can to help her break away. *No one*
deserves to be hit. An excellent resource for women in this
situation is *Say "No!" to Violence* by Mary Maracek, Director of
Respond, a shelter near Boston, Massachusetts, for abused
women. The book, available from Morning Glory Press, carries
the strong message, "You don't deserve to be hit!"

Other problems mentioned by the families interviewed for
this book include several young men deeply involved in drugs
and another young father diagnosed as manic-depressive. If
these relationships are to be saved, intensive therapy for both
partners appears needed. Reality may mean no attempt will be
made to do so.

Adolescents change rapidly as they search for their identities
and reach toward adulthood. Two young people who conceive a
child together at age sixteen may have almost nothing in common within a few years. The marriages that have the most
promise of lasting appear to be those of couples who waited
until they "grew up" before formalizing their union.

In many states, a young woman not yet eighteen needs her
parents' permission to marry. If your adolescent daughter is
pregnant and wants to marry, should you sign for her? Again,
circumstances vary tremendously. Some states require premarital counseling for all couples in which one partner is under
eighteen. Whether or not your state does so, you might decide to
give your approval only if both partners agree to premarital
counseling. Help the young couple find someone who will assist
them in looking at their readiness for marriage and at their
compatibilities and differences.

Engagement Encounter weekends help couples look at their
readiness for marriage and improve their communication. Led

by highly trained volunteers, the weekends are designed for the couple to interact almost entirely with each other rather than with the group, and can help participants in their journey toward intimacy. Started by the Catholic Church, the weekends are now available through several other denominations. For a list of denominations sponsoring Engagement Encounter in your state, contact Sue and Dave Edwards, 1509 South Forest Street, Denver, CO 80222. Telephone 303/753-9407.

If they aren't pushing marriage, but continue to see each other over your objections, what should you do? The Bradleys took the extreme measure of telling their daughter, Sarah, that she either had to stop seeing her baby's father or go live with him. When they learned Sarah was seeing Larry behind their backs, they told her to pack her clothes and the baby's things, and within an hour, mother and baby were delivered to Larry's house.

This is surely a risky technique that wouldn't work in many families, but for the Bradleys, it appears to have been effective. It took a couple of weeks of intensive interaction with the young man for their daughter to realize she wanted no part of him. She and her child are back home with her parents.

Conversely, Irene and Curtis Fletcher talked with a counselor about their disappointment with their daughter's partner. The counselor advised them not to come down hard on the relationship because often that technique backfires, driving the young couple even closer together.

Teen Fathers Need Help Too

The majority of the babies' fathers in this survey either split when they learned of their partner's pregnancy or left a few months later. A lot of unhappiness, loneliness and, judging from statistics, future poverty, can be anticipated by the young women involved. Many of the young fathers probably were not bad people. Rather, the greatest sin of most of those still in their teens was a lack of maturity.

This "sin" is pretty normal for adolescent boys in our culture. Some are simply too immature to be willing to consider their responsibility toward their child. Others would like to be responsible for their families, but how do they do that when the best jobs they can find are likely to pay minimum wage? How can the young father take the responsibility when his girlfriend's family orders her not to see him again? How can he take that responsibility if he's too scared to think straight?

Teenage fathers need help, too. They need special services to help them find jobs immediately, continue their education, and improve their job skills. They need support groups to help them look at options and deal with their feelings. These services are hard to find, and too often, the young father gets no help at all.

According to Lance Jacobs' mother, Kathleen, Lance's girlfriend, Elsa, went to Catholic Social Services for pregnancy counseling, but Lance did not. "I don't think we thought he needed anything," Kathleen mused. "As I look back, I don't think anybody tuned in to his needs. It was just 'What will you do?' and not 'What are you feeling?'

"I feel the fathers get caught between a rock and a hard place," she continued. "There's still that honor-based thing that says you have to be responsible and take care of this. Yet there is always a little knocking on the other side that says, 'You could step out of this. Nobody knows whether that's your baby.' I think they get a double message—you don't have to take care of her, but you should.

"There also is a feeling of total helplessness for the boy and for his family because the decision of whether or not to continue the pregnancy and whether or not to plan for adoption is completely up to the mother. We were kept informed, but ultimately the decision was Elsa's. You have to sit back and wait until that happens. And that's hard for the boy."

Many single teenage mothers receive no emotional and no financial support from the fathers of their babies, and the young men involved must live daily with the knowledge that they have not acted responsibly in this important area of their lives.

Some fathers don't want to parent, at least not yet. Others, however, would like to be responsible. With help, they might be able to handle that responsibility. Most, however, receive no help at all, and must handle their feelings of remorse and guilt as best they can.

CHAPTER 5

Those First Weeks— Who's in Charge?

I wanted to help. Right after Alejandra got out of the hospital, she was sick for three weeks. She was fifteen when she delivered, fifteen and hollering for Mama. Alicia Martinez, mother of Alejandra, pregnant at fourteen.

Josie was a good baby, but every time my friends called, she seemed to need something. I couldn't sit on the phone like I always had. I wanted to be a teenager. I wanted to go out with my friends, but I couldn't just get up and go any more. I felt tied down all the time. Sarah Bradley, seventeen, mother of Josie, ten months old.

The thing I probably resented the most was that Penny completely overshadowed me. I hadn't felt I got enough attention before she was born. Now I got even less. Arlana Williams, parent at sixteen.

What Kind of Help?

How much and what kind of help should you offer your
daughter when she comes home from the hospital with her
baby? If she's able to do so, it's probably best for her to take as
complete care as possible of her baby from the first because this
will strengthen the bonding between them. She will, however,
appreciate help during those early days when she's not feeling
well and the baby needs lots of attention.

A comment I've heard often from teenage mothers is, "I
needed my mom. She was too bossy, but I did need her. However, I wish she could have sometimes *asked* me instead of
telling me what to do."

Colette Adams appreciated her mother's help. "That first
month was hard," she commented. "I didn't feel good at first,
not at all, and I was grateful to have my mother. She was in-
credibly helpful. I had done a lot of babysitting so I was comfortable with Marisa, but I didn't feel that great. When Marisa
woke up at night, Mom would get up and help me. I nursed
Marisa, but I was so sore it was hard to get up that many times
every night.

"Mom taught me how to give Marisa a bath. I hadn't done
that when I was babysitting, and that's a little scary because
those little buggers are pretty slippery.

"That first week my mom bathed and dressed Marisa. When
she was about a week old, I said, 'I want her to put on the pink
sleeper.' My mom said she should wear something else, but I
said no, she should wear the pink one, and she did. Mom was
irritated, and I guess a little offended because she was trying to
help. I think I needed to clarify my role as Marisa's mother, even
to myself.

"Mom pointed out little things I didn't know, and I appreciated it. But she'd also point out little things I did know, and I'd
feel insulted."

The young mother needs support in her breastfeeding versus
bottle feeding decision. Babies thrive either way, and the important thing is for the young mother to feel right about what she's
doing. If she decides to breastfeed, perhaps because she's aware
of the advantages to the baby, she should be encouraged. If she

has problems with sore nipples or other aspects of breast-feeding, perhaps she could call the local La Leche League chapter. La Leche League is an international association of breastfeeding mothers who help other new mothers with the breastfeeding process.

Several young mothers in the interview sample mentioned boyfriends complaining the mothers were too busy caring for the babies to give them the attention they wanted. Encouraging the boyfriend to be involved in the baby's care might help. A parent's most helpful role here, as with many other problems, is simply to be a good listener.

Sometimes grandfathers fail to bond with the new baby. Diane Logan, fifteen and mother of three-month-old Leica, commented, "My dad gets mad when the baby's crying. My mom tells him to shut up. She says he did the same thing with us because he doesn't like to hear babies crying. My mom says to ignore him, that he's being protective. He's only held my baby twice." Sometimes a grandfather also feels left out when the new baby arrives. Encouraging Grandpa to interact a little more with the baby might help.

Over and over a young mother has talked about the need for her mother's help when the baby is sick. Colette Adams commented, "When Marisa was sick, Mom was invaluable. Nothing is worse than a sick baby, especially a tiny sick baby. Mom's experience with her two kids proved extremely valuable to me. Up to the time I left home, one of the greatest times to have her around was when Marisa was sick."

Those First Weeks

Dori Erickson is two months old, and her mother, Jamie, is fifteen. Jamie talked about the first weeks after Dori was born. "My mom stayed home with me the first week, and I was glad for that. I was scared, and Mom gave me lots of good pointers. I've been home alone for six weeks, and now I feel more comfortable with her.

"I breastfeed. If Mom thinks I'm doing something wrong, she tells me. She gives me advice quite often, and it's helpful. She seems to agree with about everything I do. I learned a lot about baby care at school, quite a lot of stuff my mom didn't even know after having six kids.

"I'm doing most of the care although my parents watch her when I go to work. I take her to school with me.

"We talked about it. I let them know it's my baby and I want to raise her. Everybody is going to run into times when they disagree with their parents, and they have to let them know, 'Thanks for the advice, but I think I'd better do it this way.' You have to let them know how you feel and what you expect from them. So far it's been real good. They let me raise her, but they're very supportive. It gives me a good feeling to know that if I need help, I can talk to one of my sisters or brothers or to my parents."

> *"The first week after Dori was born I stayed home, and that was a horrible week for me."*

Jamie's mother, Monica, also talked about that first month. "It's difficult not to give advice. The first week after Dori was born I stayed home, and that was a horrible week for me. I wanted to mother both of them, and I think the best thing for both of us (and for Dori) was for me to get back to work. I was having a real bad time of it at home because I wanted to take care of both of them as if they were mine.

"At one point in Jamie's pregnancy I considered giving up my job and providing daycare for her baby. I decided that would not be a good idea, and after the baby was born, I absolutely knew it would not be wise.

"But I'm finding having a baby around the house is a fun kind of thing. I'm surprised at how much Jamie has grown up. She takes good care of her baby, and I'm proud of her. She works part-time, and I babysit quite a lot. I work during the week and babysit on the weekends while Jamie's at work.

"I have lost my freedom to jump in the car and go some-where, and I resent that, but I'm dealing with it. We said before Dori was born that when we don't agree, we'll talk about it. We won't let it build. That's easier to say than do, but we're trying. Last week I was feeling upset, and I told Jamie I needed to talk

with her. I said, 'I'm doing these things for you, and this is what
I need.' I think she understood. We're trying to deal with each
thing as it comes up."

Can You Spoil a Newborn?

Some families disagree on how much to react to the baby's
cries. A generation or two ago, the "experts" were telling us to
feed the baby strictly by schedule and not to pick her up simply
because she's crying. Now the experts agree with what mothers
have always known. Babies need to have their cries answered as
promptly and lovingly as possible.

A baby can't wait for her food. Being hungry causes physical
pain that an infant should not have to endure. If she's hungry,
she should be fed.

On the other hand, a baby's cries don't always indicate
hunger, and sticking a bottle in her mouth may not be the appropriate reaction. The mother (if she's the primary caregiver) generally learns fairly quickly the best approach to her baby's cries.

Sometimes, however, other people warn the young mother
about "spoiling" her baby. Sarah Bradley commented, "One of
my aunts would say to me, 'Don't pick that baby up. Don't hold
her all the time,' but I ignored her. There is no way you can spoil
a newborn baby. She has to be held, she has to be loved."

Sometimes it's Grandma who insists the baby should be
allowed to cry. One of my students said she solved this problem
by saying to her mother, "How would you feel if you were lying
there completely helpless . . . maybe you're not hungry and you
don't need your diaper changed, but you're lonely. Would you
want to be left alone to cry, or would you want a little company?" The student reported that after that her mother didn't say
much about spoiling the baby.

Research shows that babies who are picked up when they're
crying during the early months cry *less* and exhibit more independence when they're a year old than do babies left to cry so
they'll "learn."

It's possible that the young mother may be convinced that
picking the baby up frequently is not a good idea, especially if
that young mother is exhausted and is experiencing doubts about

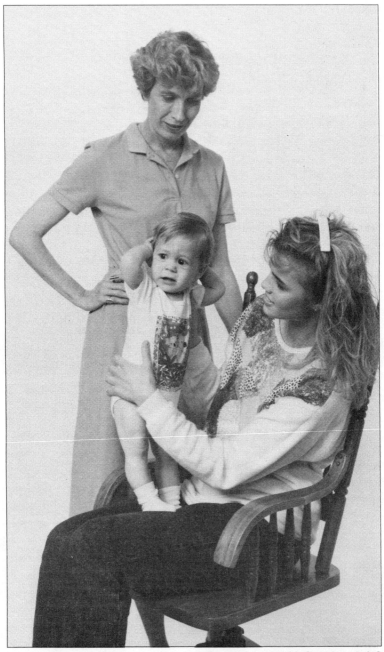

How much should Grandma help?

her parenting role. What can a grandmother do if she feels the baby is left alone too often when he's crying?

Occasionally grandma will undoubtedly pick up the baby and soothe him. However, she runs the risk of her daughter feeling she's interfering with the care of the child. The grandmother may also feel this is not her job. So how much should she push the young mother to respond more promptly to her baby?

First of all, too much nagging will only alienate a young mother already upset over her child's crying. The best approach may be to try gently to help the young mother empathize with her helpless baby, and perhaps to negotiate some additional help in rocking the baby, a task most grandparents usually don't mind too much.

The key, as always, is for the young mother to be in charge of her child's care.

If Grandma Takes Over

Who gets up with the baby that first week? If the baby's father is there, he may help. But if he isn't, do the grandparents get involved? Or should the young mother be expected to take complete care of her baby?

Alicia Martinez got pretty involved when Eric was born. "We told her this would be a big responsibility and we'd help her, but she'd have to do most of it. Then the further along she got in her pregnancy, the more excited I got. I couldn't have any more kids after Alejandra was born, and I think she sensed that I thought this was my baby.

"I think when Eric was first born, Alejandra felt pretty confused. She had said she wanted to get pregnant because she was lonesome. Then when Eric was born, I started getting up with him because Alejandra was sick. On the weekend I'd give her a rest every once in awhile, too. I got so attached to Eric that I realized I had to stop and let Alejandra do it.

"The first few months, I'd tell her how to take care of the baby, but as she went to school and learned more, she came home and told me things. She seemed to take the responsibility, and she'd tell me to butt out. It made me feel like she was growing up, being more mature."

Of course no answer fits all families. Alejandra wasn't feeling well and needed help so her mother pitched in. However, there are at least two reasons for the baby's mother, rather than Grandma or someone else, to care for the baby during those first crucial weeks if at all possible.

First, that's a critical time for bonding. Alejandra complained that Eric didn't seem to know which woman was his mother. Perhaps this started that first week when Grandma took care of him. While Alejandra needed her mother's help, at the same time it was important for her to interact as much as possible with Eric during that time.

A second reason for grandparents not doing night duty with the new baby is their own comfort. Turning into martyrs will help no one, and, if your daughter is well enough to cope by herself, this is the time to get her parenting confidence going full speed ahead.

Troy Baxter realized this, according to Javonna's mother, Marcella. "I'd start to get out of bed to get Justin when he was yelling, and Troy would grab me and say, 'No, you've got to let Javonna take charge.' That was hard for me because I had more patience with the baby than Javonna did, but I agree with Troy. For me to get up with Justin wouldn't have helped anyone."

How Much Help?

While some parents are horrified at the idea of having another baby in the house, others get caught up in the wonder of the infant. Adele Stoltz was excited when Crystal was born two months ago. She explained, "I was as happy to see Crystal as if she were my own daughter. The first week it was hard not to get out of bed each time she woke up. Carl and I would lie there listening, making sure everything was OK.

"We help Elena as much as we can during the day. I work in the afternoons, so in the morning I'll get the baby and change her and feed her and keep her with me for a little while. Elena takes care of her the rest of the day. We figure if she were married, she'd have help.

"This summer I'll take care of the baby mornings while Elena goes to summer school.

"The house is different—there's a playpen in the living room, a swing in the kitchen, and bottles in the refrigerator and on the counter. My husband and I wonder what we did before Crystal was born. When she starts crawling, we'll have to childproof the house, but we aren't concerned about that."

Elena commented, "I can go out two nights per weekend and they'll babysit, but I have to stay home otherwise. Mom mostly lets me do what I want with Crystal, but sometimes she says, 'It's too hot for that outfit,' or 'It's too cold,' or 'You should do this with her.' It really doesn't bother me because I know she's had more experience."

Stacy Bloom, whose first baby was born when she was seventeen and lived at home, commented, "I think it's terribly important that parents let you be yourself and let you handle it. Too many parents take care of it all, and then it's a shock when you get stuck with everything to do."

Stacy worked in the hospital maternity ward for several years. "There were teenage girls who came for delivery, and I'd notice their mothers did everything for the baby," she reported. "The young mothers were going to go home and be shocked when they had to take complete care of their infants."

Communicating with the Doctor

A basic problem in a three-generation household is simply "Who's in charge?" according to Richard Brookman, M.D., Adolescent Health Service, Medical College of Virginia. "In our pediatric emergency room we run into confusion as to who's in charge, who's responsible for the baby," he commented. "Of course this varies from family to family, but we often see the grandmother of the baby really raising the child while the teenage mother is back in school, back with her friends, and continuing her teenage life.

"However, if the baby is sick, the grandmother may decide it's the young mother's job to take the baby to the doctor. 'It's your baby, you take him.' So we end up with the teenage mother who isn't the primary caregiver of the child, and she doesn't have the information we need.

"'Does the child have a fever?' we ask.

"'I don't know.'

"'Did she throw up?'

"'I don't know. I just got home from school.'

"It's embarrassing for her and hard for us. If the grandmother sends the daughter in, she needs to write down the information."

If more than one person takes care of the child at home, Dr. Brookman suggests a check list similar to those used in daycare centers be utilized within the three-generation household. This can be a simple listing of care the baby receives throughout the day.

Simply jotting down the time of each feeding, diaper change and nap is a good start. The record should include any medication given the baby—kind, amount, and time given. If the baby's temperature is checked, the result should be written down. Other symptoms of illness such as vomiting need to be included.

When Baby Is Fussy

The first few months after April Hamlin was born were difficult for her mother and for her grandmother. Belinda explained, "My mom and dad were going through a divorce, and it was hard right then, but my mom was happy with the baby and gave me pointers on what to do.

"Then April started getting fussy. It was frustrating, and my mom helped me quite a bit. Sometimes I just wanted to scream because April was always crying. I breastfed her at first, then switched to formula after two and a half months. She couldn't take iron, but when we changed her formula, she was OK."

Delores remembers those first few months vividly because of April's fussiness. "Belinda is not with the baby's father, so it was just her and me and a very fussy baby," Delores explained. "April was real cranky the first three months. We were up most of the night with her. I have a full-time job, so I was working 7:30-3:30. I'd get up at 5:30 after not much sleep during the night. I felt resentful mostly toward April's father because he was never around to help Belinda.

"We agreed Belinda would have full responsibility for April, but if Belinda was sick, or if she got real tired and cranky from April being cranky, I'd take over.

"But I didn't really take over, and it's hard not to do that. I think I learned that from my mom. I was twenty and single when I had my first child, and Mom told me, 'It's your responsibility, it's your baby. I'm here to help you, but it's your baby.'"

Belinda's school provided daycare, so she took April to school with her. Belinda said, "It was great to be able to have her there. We're lucky to have that program.

"My mom took care of April like a grandma. She helped out quite a bit, and of course there is bonding between them. April's very attached to my mom. Once in awhile Mom takes care of April when she's sick, but generally I have to miss school because that's part of my responsibility. Besides, April wants me when she's sick," Belinda said fondly.

Younger Siblings Get Involved

If the teen mother is a little older, she may be able to manage baby care more easily. Angie was eighteen and a college student when Rachel was born. She recalls, "Rachel was a real good baby although she never slept through the night until she was two years old. I'm an energetic person, and I didn't feel run down and tired. I was the one who got up at night. I remember one of the first nights after I brought her home, she wakened two or three times. I was on the couch giving her a bottle, and my mom came out and sat with me, and we just talked. I appreciated that a lot."

Even in this comparatively happy situation, Angie's mother, Anita, remembers times when Angie felt her family was getting a little too involved with Rachel's care. "My two younger children were twelve and ten when Rachel was born, a wonderful age for watching a baby. I remember one time we were all saying, 'I'll get her,' and Angie said, 'Let me do it. This child doesn't even know who her mother is.'

"I looked at her and said, 'Angie, there is no doubt in that baby's mind who her mother is.' Angie felt everybody was trying to raise Rachel. I assured her that, although we did sometimes come on strong, and there were a lot of us, none of us was trying to supplant her love. Luckily Angie is basically an easy-going person."

The teen mother's siblings may want to be involved with the
baby—or they may resent its existence. In most cases, their
feelings will be mixed.

Inez Alviso commented, "It's hard at my house because I
have a lot of brothers and sisters and they say, 'The baby's
crying,' and they all get mad. They'll help me sometimes, but
when they're tired, they get mad at the baby and at me.

"Right after she was born, I felt real tired because at night
she'd wake up every two hours, and she didn't sleep much
during the day either. And I had to do everything . . . clean the
house, iron. I was walking around like a zombie. I didn't have
time for myself and I thought, 'How can I do this?' Finally I
figured out a schedule and what I could do while the baby's up. I
also tried to sleep when she would whenever possible."

The Fletchers have a son, eight, and a daughter, six, who
were excited when Carole gave birth to Kelli. They were able to
visit Carole while she was in the hospital, and they held Kelli at
that time.

Irene Fletcher commented, "I think the hardest part is our two
younger children. It's hard for them to realize there is a baby in
the house now and we need to be a little more considerate. They
want to be more involved than we'd like because Carole feels
slighted—she doesn't think she has enough time with Kelli
by herself.

"I tell her that's one of the realities while she lives here. Her
little brother and sister want to be with Kelli. At first, they would
try to get my attention when I was helping Carole. Finally I said,
'Let's let them be part of it, Carole. Let them bring the diapers,
put on her little socks, etc.'

"When you come home, you really have to let the other
children be a big part of that baby."

Postpartum Depression May Hit

Most new mothers experience some pain from their episiot-
omy the first week. If she has a Cesarean delivery, she may have
more pain. In either case, she's likely to feel tired after labor and
delivery. The tiredness will probably continue through the first
weeks when the baby is keeping her up much of the night.

Many mothers, including those who are married and planned their pregnancies, experience postpartum depression or baby blues. For a fifteen-year-old whose life has changed suddenly from carefree adolescent to new mother, baby blues can be especially intense. Again, the grandparents need to consider their own needs and their daughter's needs, and they may decide some assistance with baby care will help the new mother through this time.

Meghan Milton, whose daughter, Lorene, was born six months ago, recalled, "My first two weeks home with my baby were depressing. I felt that everyone only wanted to hold the baby when she was satisfied. Also, when my sister helped me do something, she'd argue about it. This made me so mad I'd cry.

"My boyfriend felt bad. I thought he was expecting too much of me. Then my parents—I thought they were watching with an eagle eye to see how I was taking care of my daughter. I finally figured out why I was so emotional.

"Now that I have a baby, my time is all dedicated to her. It's like being on a twenty-four hour time schedule. Whenever I go somewhere, it takes me twice as long to get ready as it used to.

"All during the night I have to get up whenever Lorene is hungry. There is no way out of it. My baby is totally dependent on me. She has made a drastic change in my life style."

"I was supposed to be in charge,
but it doesn't exactly work out that way.
I had to compromise."

Abby Peters experienced more severe postpartum depression which lasted for several months and required medication. Abby described her first somewhat grim months as a new mother:

"My mom and I never talked before I got pregnant. I'd walk in the house, get my stuff, and leave. I was doing drugs and I was all crazy. Then I got pregnant and we became best friends. Mom told me to do whatever I thought was best for the baby.

"I was supposed to be in charge, but it doesn't exactly work out that way. I had to compromise. After Latasha was born, we fought a lot because Mom acted like Latasha was hers. She would apologize and say, 'I've had kids before, and it's hard not to give advice.'

"The first week after Latasha was born was hectic. My mom was up with her sometimes. Actually, Mom's probably stayed with Latasha when she's sick more than I have. I get so frustrated and I start crying, and Mom says she'll help. I couldn't have done it without my mom. It would have been too hard.

"Latasha had colic the first three months and a lot of ear infections and congestion her first year," Abby explained. "I got to the point where I didn't even want her near me. I was crying constantly, and my teacher kept telling me I should give her up for adoption. My teacher didn't understand I had postpartum depression, and she said she was going to report me for child abuse because, when Latasha was six months old, I was smacking her hands. For a long time, Latasha and I got on each other's nerves. She could tell.

"My problem was finally diagnosed when Latasha was nine months old. They gave me medication for awhile, and now I'm OK. This year they think I'm one of the best moms at school."

Williams Family Dilemma

Arlana Williams also remembers having a tough time when she came home from the hospital. She hadn't wanted to be pregnant or have a baby, and at first she had trouble bonding with her infant. Arlana's parents, who had recently moved to a smaller house for their new life alone together, didn't want their lives changed by a baby. The result was not wonderful for anybody.

Three years after Penny was born, Arlana commented, "We came home, and three days later this depression hit me. I didn't know how to take care of a baby because I had never been around babies. I didn't know what to do, so my mom took over.

"When I was so depressed, I felt only Penny was important to other people. Friends would call and ask about her, but not about me. And my mom was taking over.

"I remember feeling outclassed by my mom. Why should I bother taking care of Penny when Mom was doing it so much better? I was afraid to try. I didn't bathe Penny for a couple of months because I was scared. Mom tried to get me involved, and she tried to teach me, but I didn't want to do it.

"My parents, of course, felt a lot of resentment. What was supposed to be their settling down, let's get to know each other again years, turned into a time of caring for another baby. And they didn't feel they could simply dump me out."

Jessica Williams' memory of those first two months is not positive either. "We brought Penny home, and Arlana did fairly well in the beginning," she said. "We hadn't been eager to have Arlana and the baby stay with us, but that was the reasonable thing to do because she had no resources and no place to go. We knew our life would be completely changed.

"Arlana had bought a crib and a changing table and fixed up her room. I vowed our home would not be turned into baby things wall to wall because I figured I had been through that. I didn't want to babytize my house. I really resented that when it happened . . . and it did.

"It was OK. I tried to help with baby care as much as I could, and Arlana resented a lot of it. She said Penny liked me best, and she probably did because I did more for her, a lot more than I ever thought I would. I vowed I wouldn't change her diapers because that was Arlana's job, and I didn't want to take over. I was afraid of getting attached to this baby and letting her take over my life, and that's what she has succeeded in doing.

"I didn't enjoy those first months, and now I think I cheated myself. I don't know what I could have done to make things different. You can't always adjust how you feel. Now (three years later) I wonder how I could ever have felt this way about this baby who is now the light of my life."

Arlana continued her story. "What could have helped?" she mused. "I could have taken more responsibility for my baby. I think the more a mother is willing to accept that this is her child, her responsibility, the better it will be at home. I think the best thing for her parents is to have the least possible amount of change in their lives, change caused by the baby.

"We tried to keep everything as much as possible confined to my room except for the playpen in the living room. Mom and Dad didn't babyproof their house. You need to spend as short a time as possible with your parents because the baby has to know who her mother is. I think there was a time when Penny thought my mother was her mother.

"If I had been forced to care for Penny, I might have bonded quicker. Or I might have placed her for adoption because I would have known I couldn't handle it. I really was very depressed, so I could have gone over the edge and done something horrible. I was close. I thought about picking up and leaving in the middle of the night.

"What probably would have happened if Mom had insisted I take care of Penny is that I'd have done it, and everything would have been fine."

Carole's Advice

Carole Fletcher, mother of one-year-old Ricki, offered good advice when she said, "Come to some kind of agreement, some kind of terms where everyone can live happily in the same house without constant conflict. I mean, sometimes me and Mom and Dad get into it, but you have to give a little and take a little. You can't always say, 'Well, I want this,' and you can't expect to live like you did before you had a child. Everything changes.

"You can't think of yourself any more. If your baby is up all night, then you have to be up all night. That's the choice you took when you decided to have the baby. You just have to be responsible for your actions, and you have to grow up real fast. With my parents, I feel if I act like a responsible adult, they treat me like one. Well, not exactly like one, but my mom and my dad both say they think I'm doing a pretty good job going to school and working and taking care of Ricki. I think they expected it of me because of the way I was before. I had always been around kids a lot.

"You have to want to make it work. If you don't want to make it work, it's not going to work at all."

CHAPTER **6**

Honeymoon
Is Over

*My mom thinks Kelli is **ours**. She's always telling me, "You'd better change her diapers," "You need to make her formula," "You'd better feed her now," and "I don't think that baby has had enough to eat." You have to take it and say, "Well, OK," and go do it. It's their house and they set the rules.* Carole Fletcher, mother at 16.

She remained a teenager with all the faults of being a teenager. Having a baby didn't cure her. Lee Williams, father of Arlana, pregnant at sixteen.

The Honeymoon Effect

Judy Snook, Social Worker, Child Protective Social Services, Adams County, Colorado, spoke of the honeymoon effect after the baby is born. "Generally the first two or three months go pretty well. The first breaking point comes soon after that. The newness is over and the routine is there. The young mother no longer gets the attention—it now goes to the baby. The grand-parents dote on the baby, and the mother is out in left field.

"At this point, the teen mother may pull away emotionally. She may go see her friends and leave the baby with the grand-parents. Being parented by the grandparents may seem safe for the baby at this point, but this can cause a lot of problems.

"My suggestion usually is, 'Let the young parent take care of the baby. If the child's safety is endangered, intervene. But model rather than take over. Grandparents have a tendency to say, 'Don't do that. Do it this way.' This tends to trigger the young parent to rebel.'"

Newness Wears Off

Six months after Josie was born, Marge Bradley noticed a change in Sarah's parenting. "At first, Sarah took wonderful care of Josie, but it's beginning to wear on her," Marge said. "The newness is wearing off. We've been home all weekend, and she needs diapers, milk, baby food. When Josie gets home from the babysitter today, Sarah won't have a bottle for her. It's as if she wants someone else to take the responsibility, and I can't do that. It wouldn't be right for her and it wouldn't be right for us. I feel she's playing this game without realizing she's doing it.

"This didn't happen at first. At first she couldn't do enough for that baby. Josie is six months old now, and over the past two weeks we have had these screaming tantrums from Sarah, 'I just can't do this any more.' She gets up in the morning, and we try to help her get away. She takes off in her school uniform and leaves Josie at the daycare center. In the evening we're generally here, but we can't trust her to go out with her friends. The latest young man is lying to her terribly, playing the game to see how fast he can get it.

"We told Sarah in the beginning that there was no way we were going to take care of the baby. Basically, we don't. She wants to be a good mother, and she loves Josie. She's a teenager and she's trying to be a responsible mother, and she's stuck.

"When Sarah was having that temper tantrum, she said she might still have to choose adoption. We responded that she might have to because we couldn't do it.

"I'm struggling in my own world to resolve things, and I don't want the responsibility of that baby. I have raised my two children almost on my own because of some problems my husband has had. We were very young when we were married.

"Mostly Sarah does a good job with Josie. I made suggestions a few times until I heard her telling her friends that I was telling her what to do. I quit doing that.

"In fact, I have acted helpless around the baby. Sarah left Josie with me one time, and she was fussing and fussing. Finally I gave her a bottle. Sarah came home and said, 'Why are you giving her a bottle?'

"'Because she was fussing.'

"'Mom, did you think of checking her diaper?' And that was it! She told friends for a long time about how helpless I was, which was fine.

"We say, 'This is a decision you've made and we'll help you, but we aren't doing it for you.' I just hope her father and I are both strong enough to carry it out."

Transition to Parenthood

Robin Gray was sixteen when she conceived, seventeen when Roni was born five months ago. Robin's transition to parenthood has been hard on her and hard on her parents.

"My life has changed. I hate having a kid," Robin complained recently. "I'm used to being on the go and I can't sit still, but now I've got to stop and take care of Roni. I can't do this. I tell other people not to get pregnant. It's one of the worst things that can happen to a teenager because you aren't a teenager any more.

"I take full responsibility for her, and I go out with my friends on weekends. If I need help, Mom's there. She and I have gotten into arguments over what I can and cannot do with Roni. I tell Mom straight out that I'll do what I want with Roni. I have friends where the grandparents have taken over the baby, and I can't stand that.

"I also can't stand it when they try to tell me what to do. They say, 'Well, you're under our roof.' Well, I'll move out. It's my baby.

"There's a lot of stress in my family, but they're doing much better than I thought they would. My little sister is like a second mother to Roni."

Robin's mother, Lois, sees reality a little differently than Robin's blithe "I take full responsibility for Roni." Lois quit her part-time job while Robin was pregnant, and she takes care of Roni while Robin works in the evenings and on weekends.

---

*"This is not what I planned to do
for the rest of my life."*

"We still aren't without problems," Lois admitted recently. "The problems aren't over as soon as the baby is born. It's an ongoing process, and we still have our battles. And when I take care of Roni, I get very, very exhausted.

"I deal with my feelings in different ways on different days. This changed our lives tremendously. This is not what I planned to do for the rest of my life. There are times when I have an easy time with Roni and I'm fine with her, but there are other times when I have had to sacrifice something I wanted to do, and at those times I have a lot of anger.

"I try to help Robin without taking full control. My husband goes to work every day, and I think that helps him accept our situation. He and I are emotional people, and this is with us constantly. We can't put it on the back shelf. It's here.

"At first Don and I argued a lot over all this. We still do, but we agree more than we used to. I have a lot of anger and resentment because he goes away each day while I'm still here. But I don't want to get out more, and I guess that's called depression. I stay right here and accept my lot."

Lois also sees Robin's relationship with her eleven-year-old sister, Tricia, quite differently from Robin's "My little sister is like a second mother to Roni."

"Tricia loves Roni a lot, but she also resents her," Lois said. "Roni has taken much of the time and attention that was Tricia's. I feel that Tricia sees it out of proportion, but she's a child, and that's the way she sees it. I go out of my way to be with Tricia and to listen to her more, but lots of times Tricia thinks Roni has priority, and of course that's because Roni is an infant. But Tricia sees it as me caring more for Roni than for her. She feels she is being pushed aside, and I don't like that. I feel this is where we need help.

"You can deal with it only to a certain point, and you need intervention from the outside. We're seriously considering going to family counseling."

"Lois and I have no time to ourselves," Don added. "It's like we're in a rush all the time, and we thought we were getting to the age where, if we wanted to go to a movie, we could."

The Grays are in a tough spot. Lois probably needs to get out of the house more. Perhaps, when Robin graduates from high school, Lois won't have to babysit so much. She needs to consider her own needs as well as Robin's.

Have Lois and Don communicated their needs to Robin? Robin says she goes out with her friends on weekends. Do Lois and Don have time each week to be with their friends or to go to the movies Don mentioned?

Robin's "Well, I'll move out. It's my baby" is an interesting comment. Are her parents encouraging Robin to work toward independence? Not as a threat, but as a reality she might prefer as soon as possible. She has a job, which is an excellent start, but she doesn't appear nearly ready to cope on her own.

Who's Going to Parent?

Maureen Morgevanne, counselor at Catholic Community Services, Denver, Colorado, feels the biggest issue is "Who's going to parent this child?" "Grandparents tend to get involved, even when it's a twenty-six year old Ph.D. who is parenting," she pointed out. "Teens have more to put up with because they are all under the same roof. Teens are ultra-sensitive, and they think people are looking for their mistakes. They need to build up their confidence and learn to believe in themselves.

"The grandparents may have unresolved anger toward their daughter. They are in the no-win position of being legally responsible for their daughter, so they feel they must take the baby in. They have a right to pressure their daughter to pick up the financial pieces, but then I see the young mother all stressed out because of her three roles—mother, student, and employee. That's hard, whatever your age.

"Sometimes grandparents give a double message. Grandma insists the young mother take the responsibility, but then continually criticizes the daughter's parenting rather than trusting her parenting abilities. It's hard to treat your teen like a capable adult when developmentally she's still a teen and she's still in your home," Morgevanne concluded.

Life with Baby

Arlana Williams' parents perhaps resented their daughter's pregnancy and the resulting changes in their lives more than any of the other families interviewed for this book. Since the time Arlana was thirteen, she and her parents have had a difficult time. At sixteen, Arlana moved out to live with her older sister, and Jessica and Lee assumed their childrearing days were over. A few months later, Arlana was home again because she was pregnant. Arlana still seemed to resent any and all rules set up by her parents, and, according to Lee and Jessica, she showed little appreciation for their help.

A year later, Jessica said, "The first three or four months after Penny was born went fairly well." (Arlana remembers those months differently. See chapter five.) Jessica continued, "Then after Penny got older, we had more and more of her things downstairs. There were diapers, there were toys, and I have trouble with that to this day. I resent having my whole life taken over by a baby.

"I finally stopped babysitting while Arlana went out on dates because she stayed out all night one time. I decided I wouldn't take care of Penny until Arlana was more responsible. So tonight she left at 9 p.m. with Penny and said she'd be back about midnight. So that's what I resent most, that and the playpen in the living room, the toys everywhere. I resent this coming into my life after I've been married twenty-four years."

Arlana shared her feelings about the same time. "At eighteen I'm still single, dating, and trying to make a life for myself. It's not fair to either Penny or me—if I had it to do over, I'd do it differently. But I don't have that chance. I'm here, and there's not much I can do about it now. I guess the best thing I can do is try to go from here and make the best of what I have, but that's hard to do.

"I don't have a lot. I don't have a good job, and I don't have much education. My parents don't want me here, I know they don't. They say they're here for me, but they don't want me, never did. It's not a nice feeling to know you aren't wanted anywhere, that nobody really wants me, nobody wants my daughter.

"Her father even denies we exist, and that makes it tough, too. I go from guy to guy, never finding anybody who really cares, who really wants to take care of us. I think marriage right now would be a mistake, but it's about the only option I have, find someone to take care of us, care about us.

"I'm standing here making food to take to the babysitter. I grind this up, tear that up, and hear Penny in the background. She's a good baby, but at times I feel like tearing my hair out."

"The teenage parent is just as resentful
of the freedom she has lost
as the grandparents are of theirs.
No longer can either do their own thing."

Arlana and Penny lived with Arlana's parents until Penny was two. At that time, Arlana was married and she and Penny moved out. Penny is now three, and Arlana's parents love her dearly— but are also delighted she's not living with them. Lee talked recently about the difficulties of three-generation living.

"We resented this baby ruining our plans," he said. "We had an idea of what we were going to do, and this was a sharp detour. The real resentment is you put all your own plans on the shelf and you get no appreciation. You may get a few hollow words but no real appreciation because the teenage parent is just as resentful of the freedom she has lost as the grandparents are of theirs.

"No longer can either do their own thing. Both the grandparents and the teen parents lose in large measure the freedom they had before the child was born.

Paternal grandma tries to help.

"I remember several times when Arlana used Penny as a bargaining tool," Lee continued. "Once, when I was denying her something, she stood at the top of the stairs saying, 'You'll never see your granddaughter again.' She was trying to use the baby to get what she wanted. She knew how much we loved Penny.

"People tend to expect that when a teenager has a baby, she all at once becomes a mature person, but that doesn't happen. Only with the responsibility of taking care of the baby does the teenager mature. We knew that if we took care of the baby, she couldn't mature, so we tried as best we could to stick by our guns and let her do things with that baby. We insisted that we not become automatic babysitters."

The Williams family is unanimous in disliking three-generation living. Hindsight is, of course, better than foresight. Apparently Arlana was not yet able to be on her own when her child was born. The most help parents can offer in such situations is to encourage as much growth toward independence for their daughter as possible. Independence doesn't mean the grandparents take care of the child so the young parent can be independent from her child. Independence for a young parent means becoming strong enough and self-sufficient enough to be the sole support of one's child, emotionally, physically, financially, the whole ballgame. It's probably the most promising goal this family could have.

Lee, Jessica, and Arlana all agree that Arlana has finally matured. She is doing a good job parenting, and she loves her child. She also speaks appreciatively now of the support her parents provided during those difficult years.

When Grandma Wants a Baby

Life in the Martinez household was quite different. Alicia and Joe had wanted several children but, because of Alicia's hysterectomy when Alejandra was three, she was their only child. Alicia had wanted another baby, and at times Eric seemed to fill that need.

"'Now give me my baby,' I'd say, and I'd hold him and rock him," Alicia recalled. "I enjoyed the crawling stage. I loved watching him. That was the fun part.

"Generally we agreed on how to raise him because Alejandra learned so much at school about babies. One time we didn't agree was when she decided to give Eric orange juice, and I said some babies can't handle it. Sure enough, he broke out.

"The baby had insurance but Alejandra couldn't get welfare because we made too much money. I used to throw it in her face about getting a job. I said, 'If you aren't going to school, get a job.' She was going to school, but sometimes her attendance wasn't all that good. I'd say, 'If you're out of school too much and get thrown out, you'll have to go to work, and then who is going to watch Eric? That's going to be a lot of money.'"

Alejandra's response was to get a job after Eric was born. She explained, "If I hadn't been pregnant, I probably wouldn't have had any responsibility, but I got a job after I had him. I faked my age (I was fifteen) and worked for six months as a waitress. My mother would always say, 'I bought this for Eric' or 'I did this,' and I wanted a job so I could take care of him. I was also going to school, and Eric was in the Infant Center. My mother took care of him while I worked.

"Once when I left Eric with Mom while I went to the movies, he wasn't there when I got home. She had taken him over to my aunt's, and he spent the night there. That upset me. She should have asked my permission.

"For awhile I don't think Eric knew who his mother was. My mother would say, 'He knows, he knows,' but I wasn't so sure.

"She would baby him. If he fell down, she'd say, 'Come to Granny.' When I lived there, Eric never came to me. He always went to my mother."

Alejandra moved out when Eric was three. She and Eric live with her boyfriend, Sal, and Alejandra is in college. Her mother misses Eric, and often drops in for an unexpected visit. Alejandra and Sal get a little frustrated, but don't see too much grandmothering now as a big problem.

To Be or Not to Be—A Teenager

Heidi Winters remembers life as a new mother four years ago when she was sixteen. "I felt different," she recalled. "I was still a kid, and here I come home with a baby. My dad kind of backed off from me, and that was hard to get used to. Just the life of being a mom, getting up to feed her, then getting up to go to school—I felt entirely different.

"I lost a lot of friends I had had in high school. I was jealous of everybody else because I still wanted to go out and be a sixteen-year-old, but I couldn't because I had Danny. I played a different role from what I really was then. I played a mama at sixteen."

Sally McCullough, head teacher for many years at the Tracy Infant Center, Cerritos, California, talked about teenagers taking the parenting role long before they or their families had expected them to do so. "Generally, the viewpoint presented at the Center by the teen mother and the grandmother was of a loving, supportive relationship within a rather stressful life style," McCullough commented.

"A positive outlook on the situation seemed to be the key to success," she continued. "Teen mothers generally demonstrated excellent parenting skills as long as the expectations were in keeping with their level of maturity."

She's Still an Adolescent

Lynn Mullen, Social Worker, Child Protective Social Services, Adams County, Colorado, says, "Let's not forget there is another side to a teen parent, the child side. Teen parents need some experiences as normal adolescents.

"My theory is that teen parents are adolescents first and parents second. They need to be encouraged to do some things that are developmentally adolescent, although they must always focus on the fact that they are parents and they have these responsibilities.

"Teen parents have a hard time focusing on whether they are supposed to be adults or they are supposed to be teenagers. They feel so out of control. I think their parents' role is to help them figure out what they're supposed to do.

"They still need limits. They may not like limits, but I think it works. Setting limits is the only way you can make their world safe. My theme is 'Let's not forget there is a child side to the teen parent.'"

*"Grandparents have to set some limits
and do a lot of guiding,
but they also have to allow some freedom."*

"It's tricky for the grandparent to monitor the development of the child plus let the mother go on with her own development," commented Judy Snook. "I think grandparents have to set some limits and do a lot of guiding, but they also have to allow some freedom. Perhaps they can provide babysitting one night each week so their daughter can be with her friends. Otherwise, the teen mom may be set up for disaster. So many grandparents say, 'You made this mistake, so no more going out. This is what you must do.' A lot of threats.

"I feel there has to be a balance, some focusing on the teenager's need for nurturing. She still needs a parent—which can make the parents feel schizophrenic. 'At one point I'll support you in growing up, and at the other point I know you need a hug.'"

Nadine and John Adams' goal for Colette and her daughter, Marisa, was for Colette's life to be as nearly "normal" as possible, while at the same time, Colette was to be the primary caregiver for her baby.

"We gave up everything for her because we felt at the time this was important," Nadine explained. "We knew we needed time alone, so we'd go out on Saturday nights, but we would babysit every Friday night and most Tuesday nights while Colette went out.

"I took care of Marisa a lot at night. Usually Colette would get up first, but if Marisa didn't go back to sleep right away, I'd go in so Colette could get her rest. I spent many hours with Marisa at night so Colette could cope and not be physically exhausted.

"But the older Marisa got, the harder it was. Or rather, the older Colette got, the harder it was. When Marisa was born, it was a piece of cake because Colette was so receptive to our help, but as she got older, she became more independent. The longer they were here, the harder it got because Colette wanted more independence—which we were willing to give to a point, but when it's your home, you need to have a say in it."

Colette attended a special school for teen parents until Marisa was eight months old. Then she returned to private school for her senior year. "The first day back was scary, exciting, neat," she reported. "My friends changed—some of my old friends had graduated, and others seemed to have different interests. But I developed a new group of friends. Connecting with male friends helped me regain trust in men. I hadn't realized how much I had lost there.

"Homework was difficult. I hated to do homework while Marisa was awake, so I'd wait until she went to sleep. My senior year I remember as being *tired*.

"I was basically a normal kid—until after 3 o'clock. My after-school time was spent a lot differently than the other kids. They did a lot of things I couldn't do.

"I didn't expect Mother and Dad to be Marisa's parents, and I didn't expect to retain the freedom I had before. So we worked together."

Both generations in this family made sacrifices in providing a loving home for Marisa. Nadine provided a generous proportion of Marisa's care, perhaps more than necessary, but this plan apparently worked well for everyone.

What About Grandma's Needs?

Katheryn Peters, daughter Abby, and little Latasha live in a two-bedroom apartment. When Latasha was a year old, Katheryn decided to give her room to her granddaughter as a first birthday gift. This left Katheryn without a place of her own.

As she talked, however, Katheryn did not dwell on the space situation. "I think the hardest thing is for the grandparent to figure out where she fits in," she mused. "All of a sudden you aren't supposed to be a parent to this child who is now a mother. She still needs guidance, but you don't want to overstep your bounds and raise her child. And you aren't quite allowed to be grandma in your own home.

"I think it's an ongoing struggle because your daughter is still growing and learning and trying different things. You have to remember you have some rights, too, in the whole scheme of things because it's your home. It's hard to sort things out, and it's an ongoing battle. Once you think you have it all straight, something else comes up and you start all over.

"It's hard for me because Latasha needed a room of her own, so I gave her mine. She sleeps better now, but I sleep on the couch in the living room and my dresser is in the hallway. Things would work out better if we each had space. There isn't a room where I can close the door and say, 'Go away.' Of course I feel resentful at times. You feel you are doing this for the people most important to you, and then you aren't appreciated.

"I think I'm probably playing the martyr role right now, putting my needs aside until Abby is through school, which is most important. Latasha is too important to put my needs first. But I'm not always this unselfish person—there are times when I resent it."

Playing the martyr generally does no one much good. One wonders why Grandma gave up her room for the baby. Did Abby want her little daughter to have her own space? If so, shouldn't Abby have given up her room, rather than her mother? Apparently, however, this was a birthday gift from Grandma to Latasha, a lovely gesture *if* martyrdom does not go along with it. But the room appears symbolic of a number of issues related to Katheryn's admission of possible martyrdom.

Communication Tips from Mother of Twins

Lawanna Edwards was sixteen when her twin girls were born eight months ago. Lawanna still lives with her parents although she left recently after an argument with them. She and the babies moved in with an aunt for a couple of days, then returned home. Lawanna shared some of the insight she has developed in trying to cope with two babies, high school, and a family that didn't expect her to have one baby, let alone two.

"I never talked good with my parents," she said. "They were supportive at first, but now they have different ideas from mine, and we have lots of conflicts. I decided I need to be here with them until I finish high school next year. When you think about moving out, you have to stop and say, 'Is it really worth it? Or is the reason you're leaving just a small thing, a little petty thing?' For me, after we finally talk out a problem, it isn't as big as I thought it was.

"When you sit and talk it out, they may understand, but they can't read your mind. They have no idea how you're feeling unless you tell them. Sometimes they may get upset, but what you have to do is give them an hour. You don't ever talk to your parents when they're upset. They don't want to hear it then, but once you give them time to cool down, it all works out.

"I've learned to tell them how I feel, then leave and not say anything else. I give them time to think about it, and usually they call me in and we'll talk about it in a sensible manner. Or I'll write down what I'm not happy with. I'll give it to my dad and he gives it to my mom, then later we talk about it."

Lawanna understands that her babies need as peaceful a home as possible. She said, "My mom would yell at me and nag at me right in front of my babies. We'd be fighting with the babies right there, and I don't like that because they'll grow up thinking, 'Why is Grandma yelling at my mother?'

"I don't like them growing up in that environment, so I tell my mom, 'If we're going to argue, let me put the babies down first.'

"At first she wouldn't, but now she says, 'When you put the babies down, I want to talk with you.'"

If the Marriage Fails

A pregnant teen may face loneliness and heartbreak when her partner leaves on hearing of her pregnancy. But sometimes it's even harder to try to save a relationship for months, only to have it end soon after the child is born.

Beth Ann Hanley, pregnant at seventeen, lived at home until Yvette was six weeks old. At that point, Beth Ann married Yvette's father and moved out. The marriage ended after three months, and Beth Ann and Yvette came back home.

The biggest problem the first six weeks after Yvette's birth, according to Beth Ann, was the fact that Yvette's father was with them a lot, and Beth Ann's parents didn't like him at all. Beth Ann's defense was to shut out her parents and do whatever Lyle wanted her to do. "He had total control over me all the time, where I went and what I did," she said.

The marriage was a disaster. Her husband abused her, and she decided to move back home. "My dad was more supportive when I came back, but my mom started taking charge," Beth Ann remembers. "At the time, I thought I did a lot (housework, childcare), but now, thinking back, I know Mom did more than half of it—now that I know what it's like to do it all myself.

"My basic advice is to get out on your own as soon as possible. I moved out when Yvette was two, and we got some help from government programs although I was never on welfare. I got food stamps which bothered me, but I was independent enough to know that would help me get on my feet to where I could totally support myself."

Peggy and Adrian Hanley talked about those two years and the adjustments the family had to make when Beth Ann and Yvette came back home:

Adrian: "We were relieved she had the strength to leave her husband, but her return created complications. We have four boys younger than Beth Ann. When she moved out, they re-arranged bedrooms and furniture. Then suddenly she was back. The house was absolutely full, not a square inch of extra space. Nobody had any privacy. Beth Ann and Yvette shared a room with our three-year-old son.

"There was plenty of room square-foot-wise, but emotion takes a lot of square footage. You could sense sometimes that people in the family just didn't like each other. They didn't like the baby, they didn't like Beth Ann being there. 'I had to give up my room, I had to give up this and that. You two have created chaos here for two years.' At times it would get pretty tense around here."

> *"I was the mom here,*
> *but she was the mom with Yvette,*
> *and I had to bite my tongue so often."*

Peggy: "The hardest thing for me was that I had always been the boss of the kids, and then when Beth Ann moved back, she was the boss of her little family. I was the mom here, but she was the mom with Yvette, and I had to bite my tongue so often. For example, I might think she should put a hat on the baby, but she didn't agree, and it was her baby.

"She would also get after her brothers for wrestling when the baby was trying to sleep. She tried to be the mother to her brothers and they didn't go for it. A lot of nights we asked the boys to go downstairs so we could talk with Beth Ann. Adrian would come home and I'd be upset, and he'd be the referee."

Adrian: "There were a lot of conversations, a lot of tears, a lot of disappointments. It took time to talk to her four brothers and help them understand the situation. Beth Ann didn't like being here any more than we all liked having her, but it was a fact of life. We'd say, 'Hey, you just have to be patient, guys.'"

Peggy: "My sister-in-law said when she came over and we would open the front door, she could feel the tension oozing out of the house."

Adrian: "The problem is you spend so much energy trying to keep the peace that you have no more energy to correct things. By the time you get tonight's mess mediated, at 10 or 11 p.m., there is no time or energy left to get anything positive going. So you get caught in one of those cages where mice are caught, and they run and run, but never go anywhere.

"The family got to the point where it was time for Beth Ann to leave. As soon as she moved out and we all had some breathing room, we were able to develop in a positive direction—but it's slow."

Peggy: "It started out with little things. She would throw some of her laundry in with mine. At first that was all right, but then I thought, 'Why should I be doing hers?' So I went out and bought a hamper and some soap and said, 'This is yours.'"

"I helped take care of Yvette for a few months while Beth Ann was at work. There were days when I felt trapped and that's why I finally said to Beth Ann, 'I don't want to do this. I don't want to be a babysitter.' I decided I wanted to be a grandmother, and she managed to get Yvette into full-time daycare. Yvette needed to have Grandma and Grandpa be her buddies, and we couldn't do that when we were bringing her up part of the time.

"It was a little easier for me because I work away from home. I would leave the house each day, so I had that opportunity for escape. I think this gave me more tolerance that it would work out in the long run. But that doesn't bring problems to any resolution, so I have had to be a little more assertive. I found in trying to give Beth Ann positive direction, I had to be a little tougher than I was at first."

Adrian: "It finally got to the point where we said, 'We love you very much, but it's time for you to go.' Financially, she's strapped, but she does a good job of managing. She pays her bills and she pays her rent. She almost lives within her budget."

Handling the Hard Times

Delores and Guy Hamlin were divorced two months before sixteen-year-old Belinda's baby, April, was born. Delores and Belinda moved into an apartment. Their relationship is fairly good now that April is seventeen months old, but Delores discussed some rough times:

"Belinda still has some growing up to do. She has to learn that April is her baby, and that the baby comes first in her life. There were a couple of times when Belinda decided to run the streets until 3 a.m. I took April and let Belinda run. Then I locked her out of the house and told the landlady not to let her in under any circumstances.

"She was gone for a week. I knew she was with friends and that she was all right, but that was hard.

"After a week of that, Belinda decided it wasn't peaches and cream out there. She came back, we talked about it, and settled back into our routine.

"Belinda took off a second time, and this time she took April with her. She was with the same girlfriend, a young woman with lots of problems of her own. I did the same thing—didn't let her back in the house until she was ready to talk. She had people call my house and say, 'Belinda needs money for diapers. She needs clothes for April.'

"I'd say, 'No, she needs to come home.'

"I worried constantly about them, but I felt this was Belinda's decision. I didn't go after her, call her, or check up on her. She called me collect one night and said she needed some money. I said, 'No, you have to come home and talk to me first.' She hung up on me, and that hurt.

"Belinda came around a couple of days later and said, 'Mom, I don't know what's wrong with me.' I think she was having trouble with April's father.

"I guess she was having a hard time facing the fact that she had a baby and she couldn't go run the streets any more. She said she was upset about that, wondering where she would go, wondering if she and Jerry would ever get back together, and she kind of took it out on me.

"But we sat down and talked when she came home, and things have been OK since. She was hoping Jerry would come back into her life. He didn't, and that was hard for her to face. She didn't know how to handle that."

A tough love approach is hard for most parents, but sometimes it is the most loving and caring approach. There is a continuum between drastic measures such as this and not doing anything about problems, and each family must find its own place on that continuum.

Melissa's Advice

Melissa Baird talked about Blake's early months: "He was a good baby, but when he started walking, put him back!

"The first couple of weeks were OK, but as he got older, Mom would say, 'I'd do it this way . . .' When Blake was only two months old, the babysitter said all the kids there were coming down with the chicken pox. I just wasn't ready for the chicken pox. I called the doctor, and he said Blake probably wouldn't catch it if I kept him away from the other kids for a few days. So I stayed with him that week, and my mom freaked out because I took a few days off work. Work comes first with her, always.

"Other times when Blake was sick, I felt I should be home taking care of him, but my mom didn't. We'd argue over that a lot. We'd argue over little things."

During the past three years, Melissa has thought a lot about making three-generation living work. She advises other teenagers, "You have to respect your parents because they have opened their home to your baby, and you shouldn't take advantage of it. You have to remember they don't owe you anything. You owe them for helping you.

"I think a lot of teenagers don't take on the responsibility for their child. That's happened with some of my friends. They feel resentful because they don't feel they have a life of their own anymore, so they leave their responsibility and go out partying. What they don't realize is they still won't be happy. Going out is just pushing everything away."

Melissa also has suggestions for grandparents. She says, "Remember that your daughter has a life, too. She has her own opinions and her own feelings, and you have to respect that. Forcing your opinion on somebody causes tension. You need to have faith that your child will make the right decisions. If you don't, they feel it. That has a lot to do with the way a teen handles things, how she reacts. The more you push your kids, the more they want to back away. Everybody needs their space, and the more you try to invade, the more they will push you out. The more you push, the madder she may get, and then, well, 'I'll show them.'

"When you're a teenager, you rebel, whether you're a mother or not. Parents who keep their mouths shut probably get further with their kids than those who constantly nag."

A grandparent said facetiously, "Advice for parents? Run away from home and leave no forwarding address!"

Most parents don't resort to running away because their daughter is or will be a parent-too-soon. If the three generations will be living together, their greatest challenge lies in balancing the care of the child with the needs of the young mother and the needs of the grandparents. For some families, the concept of tough love may be needed. Hopefully, however, the team approach and good communication between the generations will achieve a balance that works—most of the time—for everyone.

CHAPTER 7

Support and Help
Are Available

My mom suggested I go to Children's Home Society for counseling. That was probably my life saver. I went once a week and talked out my problems with my counselor. She was wonderful. Angie Todd, pregnant at seventeen.

One of the best things my parents and I did was to get counseling. That brought us all together. There was a lot of crying, and I think that helped. We learned how important it is to be open with each other. My mom and I said very unkind words to each other, but we talked it through. Maggie Hertzel, pregnant at nineteen.

If you can't handle the situation, go talk to somebody, other parents, or find a support group. It's important to get your daughter involved in any special services. Is there a special school program? Go talk to the teacher. Belinda's teacher was super. Delores Hamlin, mother of Belinda, pregnant at fifteen.

Families in Crisis

For many families, coping with a too-early pregnancy is
definitely a crisis. Most need support, whether from a friend
who is good at listening, a clergyperson, counselor, support
group, or other helping person(s). The important thing is to get
the needed help because talking about a difficult situation often
results in problem solving, moving from an "Ain't it awful"
stance to "This has happened, and we will deal with it the best
we can."

Judy Peterson is a bright, hard-working, sometimes funny
person who founded and directs BETA (Birth, Education,
Training and Acceptance), a comprehensive program for pregnant and parenting teens in Orlando, Florida. Peterson elabo-
rated on her counseling techniques:

"So often, families coming in are in real crisis. They're angry
that their daughter has betrayed them, and they have an overwhelming sense of failure, thinking they have done something
wrong. Family issues that have been on the back burner for a
long time and which have nothing to do directly with the pregnancy, affect the way they deal with the pregnancy.

"I can only do what people allow me to do. Sometimes all it
takes is me sitting there while the family battles it out. The first
thing we have to do is help take off some of the pressure. If
Mother is very, very involved, we help her back off a little. Dad
is often more removed. He may feel confused and think he's
losing his place in the family to some extent."

A pregnant teen may see Peterson several times before her
family is involved. The young woman is probably trying to find
her independence, her identity, and may already be in the
process of breaking away from her family. This pregnancy may
be seen as a failure, an event that will keep her from going out
on her own as soon as she'd like.

"Basically, I deal with the teen's feelings of dependence,
failure, hurt. If the relationship with her partner is over, she's
suffering at two levels, the loss of her partner and the pain she is
inflicting on her family," Peterson pointed out.

"Then we deal with Mom and Dad. Dad may be very, very
angry, and Mother may just cry. So often, Mother sees herself as

having failed as a mother, having failed her family. You let the steam off a little, and everybody settles down.

"At this point, we bring the family together. At first, Mother may take charge with the daughter acquiescing, and the father may be withdrawn and angry. We move from that point to ways of establishing communication within that family. So often, a great deal of love is there, but has been pushed aside in the process of the children maturing."

Empowerment for Daughter

"We work with the parents on giving back some control to their daughter," Peterson explained. "We help the daughter learn how to solve problems within the family without losing her independence. There's a lot of empowerment involved with family counseling.

"An issue we have to cover with many families is that there comes a point where their child has a right to her private life. There comes a point where you don't check her contraceptive drawer and she doesn't check yours."

After parents realize they have not failed their child, how can the situation be resolved? What does the family want? "This is not the parents' baby," Peterson continues. "The more they try to take control, the more the teenager will act out." The teen is trying to gain control, and Peterson suggests the parents empower their teen rather than try to hold on to the power themselves.

"What do you do when the power runs out?" Peterson asks. "You try to move out of the power stance into a partnership stance. With power, perhaps you can stop a child's poor behavior by threatening him. But even if you stop the behavior, you haven't taught that child how to handle himself. We try to help parents help their child grow into independence through skill building."

Skill building covers a wide array of tasks from learning how to make formula to acquiring job skills which will enable the young parent to support herself and her child.

Good communication requires skill building for most of us. Who is going to babysit? What are the rules for going out? How is the housework shared? "You're still dealing with a teenager, and you're probably dealing with a teenager who is having a difficult time growing into maturity," Peterson explains to her clients. "Often the baby simply exaggerates the problems. Sometimes the parents have trouble controlling their daughter, and then they try to control the baby, too.

"Basically, that's her baby. If you're going to move the power issue to her and her baby, you have a real problem," Peterson cautions.

If the teenage parent is going to grow into the power she needs to manage her life and her baby's life, she needs to be included in negotiating the rules. This negotiation needs to start while she's still pregnant. (See chapter eight.) For negotiations to work, teen and parents must each respect the others. They may disagree, but they don't need to put each other down as individuals.

---

*"Don't be afraid to let your child
become a participating member of the team."*

Parents, however, also need to know where their daughter is developmentally. A fifteen-year-old who has a child is probably quite unrealistic. She has not yet developed abstract reasoning or much ability to look into the future. "You're going to ask her to take charge of her life, and she is not going to have the skills to do this," Peterson points out. "It will be a balancing act. Let the teen explore how she feels without directives and ultimatums.

"If people use a little humor, it can help. If it gets too hot and heavy, declare a recess. Let everybody retire to a neutral corner until everyone is over the urge to strangle each other," Peterson suggests.

"Don't be afraid to let your child become a participating member of the team. When the parent disagrees, perhaps she can say, 'Why don't you think about it? This really makes me nervous. Maybe you can think of something that won't make me so nervous.'"

Peterson concludes, "Each member of the family needs to understand that for there to be order in any system, there must be things people agree on, and there must be certain responsibilities. The first thing parents need to understand is that children fail at these tasks. That's why they need parents. You have to keep coming back to the issue and communicating the issue. Over time, things change although, unlike television, everything is not solved by the commercial."

A helping person, whether a counselor, teacher, support group leader or member, or simply a friend, can help a family negotiate, because the helping person can step outside and see what everybody needs.

Grandparent Support Group

Carolyn and Andy Stefaniw participated in the first grandparent support group sponsored by BETA almost five years ago. Now they and another couple lead the monthly support meeting.

"How do we help? We tell our story and hope that we can help people who feel they're the only ones with this kind of problem. You feel like the whole world is pointing a finger at you, and talking with people helps us," Carolyn explained.

"Our daughter lived at BETA while she was pregnant. With help from BETA, we did some negotiating before she came home, and we stuck by our guns after the baby was born. Our rules weren't very difficult to follow. Number one, you go to school. Number two, you have a job. Number three, keep a reasonable curfew. Number four, take care of your room. We agreed to simple rules, and we said they would have to work. In the beginning, going to school and working part-time was a problem every once in awhile because Suzanne was only sixteen, but she knew her responsibilities.

"It was hard sometimes to remember that we are the grandparents, and she is the mother. That's the problem we see with a lot of the newer people who come into the group. The grandmother wants to take over. Sometimes the grandmothers really want to take this little baby and have a second chance, but we see that as a detriment for the mother of the baby because she doesn't grow."

The BETA grandparent group has a few simple rules, too, according to the Stefaniws. "We respect each other's privacy.

Whatever we say in that room stays there. Even with our daughters, we don't use names, we don't get specific. Also, we don't make each couple feel like they have to talk. When they're new, they're scared. We'll ask, 'Do you have anything to say this evening?' If they don't, that's OK. Then when they do open up, it's likely to be a flood.

"We've done some outreach in the churches here, but we're strictly non-denominational, and I think that's important," Andy concluded.

TAPP Offers Support

The Teenage Parent Program (TAPP) in Louisville, Kentucky, started a grandparent support group several years ago, one of the first in the country, according to Georgia Chaffee, TAPP principal. She recalled, "The grandparent group came out of our experience in 1982 when we were working with the Ford Fatherhood Project. Fathers were fine, but we felt we also needed to help parents of the teenage parents. I put that in as an added component, a group for the parents of the young mothers at our school and the parents of the boys in our evening fatherhood project."

Family support groups, which also include a sibling support group, meet weekly at TAPP. "At first we thought we'd concentrate on skill teaching, particularly in the area of baby care, in the grandparent group. Then we learned that these grandparents had needs of their own, and they wanted to deal with those needs," Chaffee remembers.

Each group is led by a social worker who follows up during the week with home visits as needed, and who is on call if a parent wants to talk. In addition to the all-important sharing, each meeting ends with the teaching of one skill dealing with communication, nutrition or other relevant issue.

"We ask them to practice that skill, then report back the next week," Chaffee explained. "The reporting back is important because that encourages them to make a commitment.

"Over and over we hear from parents, 'I don't think I could get through this without the support group at TAPP,'" Chaffee added.

TAPP offers an intensive intake process in which the pregnant teen is introduced to each component of the TAPP program. "When she gets to the family component, we offer to enroll her family in the support groups. We follow this up with a call to her home," Chaffee said.

Bill and Ethel Mae Young were as devastated as anyone could be when they learned their sixteen-year-old daughter was pregnant. Ethel Mae remembers going with Luanne to the TAPP school the first time. "We walked in that day with heavy hearts and tears and lumps in our throats," she said. "It was very hard, something I didn't want to do. But when we walked into TAPP, the atmosphere was so warm and loving, I felt immediately that we had help. This school is marvelous. They are always supportive. They are there for the girls, for the babies, and for us, too.

"Going to their support group helped tremendously. Luanne's pregnancy is something we didn't want to happen in our family, but it happened, and there couldn't be a better place for our daughter and for us than the TAPP school."

Importance of Open Discussion

Community Maternity Services (CMS), Albany, New York, also coordinates groups for the parents of teenage parents. The groups meet weekly to voice and share their concerns and feelings about their daughter's pregnancy and care of the child.

Meetings contain an open discussion time as well as presentations on communication skills and other issues. Some of the problems addressed include:

• Getting used to the new role of grandparents
• Helping the teen mother take responsibility for her child
• Communicating with the teen father and his family
• Coping with new financial burdens

For fourteen years, therapists Shirley Scholsberg and Neal Cervera have been leading the CMS group for parents of teenage parents. Participants usually join the group when their daughter is pregnant, and may continue in group as long as they wish. Sometimes the parents of the teen father participate.

Parents often continue in the group after the child is born because they need to talk about rules and boundaries, the shock of having the third generation at home, and how to support young parents who can't do it all themselves.

"Parents look at their shock and grief, their rage and anger. As they get through that crisis, they look at how they can use these experiences so they can have a better relationship with their daughter (or son) after the baby is born," Scholsberg explained. "Some of our teenage clients come from families with a history of multiple crises, and they seem to settle down during pregnancy. This is a good time to do crisis work, and the pregnancy truly is a crisis. The grandparents come for help in dealing with this crisis.

"The grandparents must maintain their grandparent role rather than slip into the parenting role."

"Sometimes we see ambivalently bonded grandparents whose kids are acting out and having a baby," Scholsberg continued. "A lot of work can be done with this group through helping them realize this is perhaps their final opportunity to recreate some family closeness. Neal and I are convinced these girls need a strong support system at home, but at the same time, the grandparents must maintain their grandparent role rather than slipping into the parenting role."

Scholsberg said her agency is seeing more and more children in court placement who spent the first two or three years with Grandma, then went back to Mother. Too often, when the child is an adolescent, the mother can't control her. "In group we try to help the grandparent realize who has to bond with the baby. They have to back away themselves and support the teen bonding with her baby.

"The biggest thing some families have to work on is how to pull back, to realize they must not take care of the baby because their daughter must assume full responsibility. If they step in and take care of the baby, the teen mother will back away. The group is especially good for these parents because they get a lot of support from each other on how difficult it is to be grandparents when some of them are still young enough to be parents.

"If the girl returns home with her baby, grandparents must let her set the rules and make the mistakes they might have made at her age," Scholsberg cautioned. "They need to imagine she is on her own, because then she would have to make these mistakes. She must make the decisions, good or bad, because that's how she grows. Otherwise, she remains a child, a child taking care of a baby.

"The grandparents need to be clear that their daughter's role has changed dramatically. She is no longer a child, she is a mother," Scholsberg stressed. "There will still be rules around the house, but she must make the rules for the baby. We talk about the great importance of the baby bonding to the primary caregiver, but s/he doesn't need to bond to everybody. We encourage the grandparents to get busy and start enjoying life, and we remind them that grandparents are the ones who enjoy the kids and don't discipline them."

Benefits of Group

Neal Cervera, co-facilitator of the CMS group, authored "Group Work with Parents of Unwed Pregnant Teens: Transition to Unexpected Grandparenthood" (*Social Work with Groups,* Volume 12, Number 1, 1989). He writes on page 75, "The underlying theme in a parents' group is mutual aid. Group work provides a forum to stimulate thinking, release some powerful feelings, and explore alternatives."

Cervera describes three stages parents work through as they participate in the CMS group meetings. During the engagement phase, parents new to the group tend not to want to discuss their family's dilemma. Group leaders and participants can help them express their pain and uncertainty so that problem solving can begin.

Next comes the "working through" stage. It is at this time that the twin themes of loss and attachment to the baby appear, according to Cervera. During this stage, parents often feel overwhelmed and confused about this new role they must assume. They had not intended to become a grandparent under these circumstances, but it is during this phase they begin to explore the meaning of doing so.

"Although new members hear the word *grand*parent, it is not until there is a lessening of hostile feelings that a parent can assume the *grand*parenting role," Cervera states on page 88. "Group process helps the parents to express their love towards their grandchild and daughter as well as ventilate their feelings of anger, blame, guilt, shame and sadness." As this happens, the grandparents-to-be begin to focus on the realistic issue of preparing for the coming baby.

During the "resolution" phase, according to Cervera, the grandparents may actively free themselves of hostile feelings and attach themselves to the baby and to their daughter. At this time in group, there is also a reinforcement of the limits that were set earlier with the daughter. This is done to help the grandparents avoid the danger of overextending themselves in caring for their daughter's child.

Carman and Warren Boltz have been attending the CMS grandparent group for more than a year. They talked about the benefits they feel they received:

Carman: "I was committed to that group because I knew having Lupe and her baby living with us would never work unless we had some help. The counselors have been invaluable. I know it would have come to fever pitch and Lupe would have left by now if we hadn't had that support group.

"This is an extremely difficult situation, and I think parents need help. Someone needs to help you stay on the straight and narrow, just to keep things sane, to give parents guidelines as to what might work."

Warren: "Part of being with the group is listening to other folks share their experiences and realize we aren't unique. Listening to the way they work things out helps us. CMS requires their teen clients' parents to attend the grandparent group meeting three or four times, and some people come into the support group kicking and screaming. But I notice those who stay tend to change their attitudes. It's quite obvious they do better with their family situation than if they hadn't come to these meetings.

"One of my biggest fears was that Carman would turn out to be the mother of the baby rather than Lupe. Lupe, like most young ladies her age, will let other people do as much as they will do. Carman is so loving, especially with babies, that I figured she would want to take over the parenting, and then Lupe wouldn't take the responsibility. Lupe will go out on her own one day, and I want her to be as normal a mother as possible.

"Group has helped on that, and I think Carman has committed to being a grandparent, not another mother. Sometimes we bite off pieces that really belong to Lupe, but not as much as we would have without that formal learning process in group."

Value of Mediator

In most areas, a support group such as the ones described here are simply not available. What then?

Delores Holmes, Director of Our Place, Family Focus, Evanston, Illinois, stresses the need for a third party to help the family sort out and deal with the various issues they're facing. "I think there ought to be a mediator to help them hear what each is saying to the other. I think we all have problems within our own households with communicating. Short term counseling would be helpful because that would let a mother hear there is a cry under that rebellion, and let the daughter hear the mother is not abandoning her.

"The mediator doesn't have to be a therapist or a social worker. It can be someone from your church, perhaps your next door neighbor, someone you both agree on, someone who can help you hear each other. This can be a beginning.

"In the best of all possible worlds, we'd get counselors to play this role, but not all of us will have a counselor available to help," Holmes pointed out.

"The mediator needs to help the grandparents and teen mother work it out in the beginning. The grandparents need to set the guidelines—'we want to share in this, and this is what we'll do. We want you to attend some school ball games, perhaps some dances, but it won't be every weekend.' Or 'We'll babysit on Saturday night, and that will be your night out.' That negotiation has to happen if you're giving her the responsibility of being a parent. You give her guidelines, you help her understand this is what it's all about," Holmes concluded.

An Almost-Adoption Plan

Anita Nolan had been divorced a year and was attending
college full time when her seventeen-year-old daughter, Angie,
said she was pregnant. Anita's two younger children still needed
her, and Anita wondered if she would have to give up her new-
found independence to take care of a grandchild. She decided to
talk with a counselor in the Women's Center at the college.
Anita talked about the counselor and the influence this woman
had on her reaction to the coming grandchild:

"Leona Hafner is a strong woman, divorced, certainly a role
model for me. Sometimes her advice seemed a little harsh, but I
come from a sheltered environment where my needs were not
supposed to be important. Leona would say, 'You need to stay in
school. This is Angie's problem.' I have always been a rescuer—
you've got a problem? I'll handle it for you. Leona helped me
break out of that pattern.

"At that time, all I could do was cope with running my own
home and my own life. Angie was talking to a counselor at
Children's Home Society, and I felt she was in good professional
hands. It was probably good that I was so busy I didn't have
much time to think.

"Leona was telling me Angie should make an adoption plan.
To this day, Angie doesn't know I had misgivings about that. I
would tell her that as long as I had a roof over my head, she
could stay here. But her father had some serious health problems, and I knew my spousal support could end at any time. We
could have been out in the street so fast your head would swim.

"I had to say to Angie, 'If something happened to your dad,
how could I provide for you and a baby?' Of course that was
motivating me to go to school and to talk tough to Angie. I was
saying, 'You can't count on me or your father to provide your
security.' That was the tough talk, the tough love.

"We got no verbal support for adoption from anybody close
to Angie. Her older brothers who didn't have regular jobs said
they would 'help out.' Sure, they'd help.

"For nine months Angie's father wasn't around. Then when
she was in the hospital, he told her he and his new and pregnant
wife could take the baby with them. Talk about enabling . . .

with one comment like that he was undoing all that Children's Home Society had done. It had to be her choice, and it was."

At delivery, Angie still wasn't sure about adoption. After Rachel was born, Angie held her and fed her. She was still considering adoption, and had decided to place Rachel in temporary foster care while she made up her mind.

One evening when Rachel was five weeks old, Anita discovered Angie standing in the living room crying. "What's the matter, Honey?" she asked.

"Mom, I don't think I can do it."

"Do what?"

"Give her up," and Angie cried harder.

Anita continued her story:

"I realized we just hadn't dealt with it. I looked at her and said, 'That's OK. We'll manage somehow.'"

Anita told Angie she was not going to raise the baby. She would not be a rocking chair grandmother. "I had been married since Day One, I reared five children, and I didn't remember anything except my life of raising kids. I was finally taking care of me. It was my turn now. I would not be waiting in the rocking chair.

"'If you keep this baby, it's yours to feed, to change, to get up with at night,' I told her. We put all the baby paraphernalia in Angie's room. Angie had one-hundred-percent care of Rachel. I was there as the older experienced person, but I didn't hop up to heat bottles. I guess I was in an advisory position. Angie got her own babysitters, interviewed them, and made her selection.

"She applied for AFDC (Aid to Families with Dependent Children), which she hated. But for that first year, that was the only way she could handle her responsibilities. She continued going to college.

"From the moment she told me she wanted to raise Rachel herself, I turned immediately to knowing we would cope."

Rachel and Angie stayed with Anita for two years. Then Angie and Rachel's father were married.

Anita still feels going to the Women's Center at her college and talking with Leona Hafner helped her cope with the crisis of Angie's pregnancy.

Sources of Support

When they have a problem, many people turn to their church
for support. They may call their clergyperson and request
counseling time. They may be able to share their feelings in a
small group within their church. Several people interviewed for
this book talked about the help they received within their
church. Some had expected condemnation, but found instead
love, support, and caring.

One of the couples spoke highly of the help they received
from their pastor, Russ Mueller, St. Timothy's Lutheran Church,
Lakewood, California. Pastor Mueller commented, "As a
church, we need to be very open. I was simply someone they
could come to and unload. I listened and they knew I listened.
I was concerned.

"As they felt free to lay out their concerns, they were able to
look at them and come up with some decisions. I didn't give
them any great assistance in terms of advice, but I helped them
lay the problem out and come up with some solutions."

Young parents and parents-to-be sometimes find the support
and the love they need within their church family. Stacy Bloom
said, "My friends at school turned away while I was pregnant,
but my friends at church are still my friends today. Parents, too.
When parents of my school friends found out, it was like you
can't hang around her any more, but the parents at church
accepted me. They gave me a shower at church, and more than
eighty people came. My church probably kept me in focus as to
what to do. I always felt Patrice was my responsibility, and I had
to take charge."

Judy and Jim Glynn, Axtell, Kansas, are birthgrandparents—
their daughter released her infant for adoption several years ago.
During their daughter's pregnancy, Judy and Jim, as well as their
daughter, received counseling support from a Catholic Social
Service counselor in a nearby city, but they found little formal
support in their own community.

Because of this experience and her awareness of other
people's needs, Judy Glynn and the Social Concerns committee
of her church created the "Like-to-Like Ministry." Like-to-Like
Ministry offers people the chance to talk with another person in

confidence, a person who generally has experienced a stressful situation *like* their own. "We realized we needed to reach out to people undergoing crises, and we knew we could never sustain support groups in all the needed areas because we're a small rural community," Glynn commented.

In addition to teenage pregnancy, Like-to-Like offers support to people in other kinds of crises such as alcohol and drug dependency, bankruptcy, divorce, serious illness, and other problems. Volunteers receive eighteen hours of training and commit to serve a year at a time.

Participants in the training learn basic communication skills such as active listening, use of "I" statements, and how to carry out the initial contact with the client. The Like-to-Like Ministry has developed a training manual for these sessions.

Sponsored by the Nemaha-Marshall Catholic Regional Council, the Like-to-Like Ministry is open to all faiths, both as volunteers and as clients. "Like-to-Like volunteers do not provide counseling or give advice to solve the problem. What they can give is to listen and provide information about available resources," Glynn explained. Three professional counselors are available, not only for backup if the volunteer feels the client needs additional help, but also to answer questions the volunteer might have. For more information concerning this kind of individual support, contact Judy Glynn, 913/736-2713.

Counseling Resources

Mike Chilver is a school guidance counselor. He also works with the Break Through Program for High Risk Youth in Orange County, California. He identifies communication and the validation of self-esteem as the two key issues in his work with families. He highly recommends support groups for parents and for teenagers.

"I think kids and family members need to get involved," he explained. "The more they isolate themselves, the more their problems intensify. When you're isolated, you tend not to think things out in a logical way.

"If your daughter is going through an emotional crisis, as most adolescents are, encourage her to get involved in a support group with other young parents her age so they can share ideas and information," Chilver stressed. "Sometimes parents are the last people adolescents want to listen to, and a support group of their peers can be extremely helpful."

When Beth Ann Hanley came back home after a disastrous three-month marriage, Beth Ann realized she needed counseling. "I was doing lousy emotionally," she recalled. "My husband had abused me emotionally and physically. There were times when I knew there was an easy way out. I could dump the baby on my parents, and I did that too many times. I'd say, 'Mom, I can't handle this. You take the baby,' and I'd leave.

"I had a real feeling I had nothing going for me. What was I going to do with my life? I went into counseling, lots of it. Finally, things started to soak into my head, and I decided I wouldn't let myself go through this any more. It was time for me to pick myself up and do something with my life."

For information about local support groups, contact a United Way non-profit counseling service, local community college, Family Services Association, Mental Health Services, and/or the Department of Public Social Services office. There is help out there although such help is limited because of the lack of adequate funding and the increasing need for services.

If you'd like this kind of support, try to find a community service agency close to home. If there is no support group for young parents or for their parents in your area, perhaps you can work with the director of an existing agency. You could explain the need, and perhaps help get a support group going.

"Professional help is hard to get when you're hurting so bad," Jessica Williams commented. "I was so lonely and so lost. I had to start someplace, and I found Children's Home Society in the phone book. You don't know what your own feelings are when you're so upset. You have to find somebody who will let you heal."

Whether you choose counseling, a support group, or sharing your feelings with a peer, you'll find you aren't alone in the challenges you face. Knowing you aren't alone often is the first step toward working through the problems and supporting each other as a family.

CHAPTER 8

Who Picks Up
the Diapers?

*We're slobs, both Danny and me, and I suppose he gets it
from me. I'm terrible in my own room, but most of the time
before we leave, we pick everything up and put it in our room.
If I don't, the minute I wake up in the morning, my mom
starts yelling.* Heidi Winters, twenty, mother of Danny,
almost five.

*Arlana's room was as much a disaster after she had the baby
as it was before. She was still the same teenager as she was
before she gave birth.* Lee Williams, father of Arlana, pregnant
at sixteen.

*When Arlana was living here, she wouldn't even pick up her
own stuff, let alone the baby's things. I'd come in the door, see
the mess, and completely lose it.* Jessica Williams, Arlana's
mother.

"Clean Your Room!"

Teenagers have a reputation for being messy.

"Don't you leave this house until your room is clean."

"I can't stand this mess. Get in there *right now* and take care of it."

All over the country, mothers are demanding that their sons and daughters clean their rooms, and those sons and daughters are resisting. In my own family, we used to read her daily horoscope to our teenage daughter. We tried ending the reading with "and clean your room." It worked for a couple of days. The only real cure for her was moving out. When she got her own apartment, she suddenly was able to keep her home beautifully clean and neat.

Most parents have to deal with messy kids. Babies add to the mess simply by being there. Toddlers bring their toys to the living area, play for a few minutes, then dump them and bring out more. Preschoolers and older children may, if properly encouraged (nagged?), become fairly helpful in keeping a home liveable. Then, in many homes, the battle starts again when those children become teenagers. Rebellious teenagers are not likely to clean their rooms quietly between other battles with their parents. Those teens who are not blatantly rebelling may still drive their parents crazy with their sloppiness.

Teens tend to be busy. For some, it's participating in school, church, sports, and/or community activities. They may be working, or they may spend a lot of time on homework. For many others, time slips away as they hang out with friends or shop at the mall. When they're home, they may seem tired all the time. For whatever reason, cleaning their rooms and doing their share of other housework has low priority for many teens.

Baby Adds to Teen's Clutter

These normal problems may be tremendously magnified if the teenager has a baby. Combine typical teenage behavior with the needs of an infant, and the result is not likely to be the TV commercial version of the spotless home.

Carole Fletcher, eighteen, feels she does fairly well in this department. "They get mad when my room isn't all picked up

and neat," she said. "My mom gets mad if I don't take the
diapers out of the diaper pail every night. I try to keep after
myself. I know it's my responsibility, and I don't want her to do
it. I take care of Kelli because I want her to grow attached to me
rather than to my mom.

"My mom does the washing, and sometimes we have arguments over that. My mom says, 'I have to do all the laundry,'
and I say, 'Let me do it,' and she sighs and says, 'No, I'm
doing it.'"

Carole's mother commented heatedly, "My biggest problem
is Carole. Her room is a disaster. She doesn't like to pick up
after herself, and now she leaves baby clothes around, she lets
the diapers lay. She uses disposables, and I say, 'Carole, those
diapers belong in a bag outside.'

"Just this morning I said to my husband, 'There are diapers
on the basement landing this morning. Can't she see?'

"Carole is eighteen, and I'm not going to nag any more. So
I shut her door. But when I start picking up after the baby,
I get upset."

Alicia Martinez also talked about Alejandra's sloppiness.
"The big fight we had all the time was her not cleaning up after
herself," she said. "Alejandra was the biggest slob, she was
scum. It was like she would do things just to bother me. I would
yell and scream and stand right beside her and make her pick up
her stuff.

"Nothing worked. A couple of times I took everything out
and threw it in the trash. Her response was, 'I don't care. I don't
have anything anyway.' The only solution would have been to
put her in her own place . . . or in cold storage. Now that she's
living with Sal, she seems normal again."

Looking back, Alejandra's mother wonders if perhaps
Alejandra was anemic. She always seemed tired and bored. Any
mother of an infant or a toddler, of course, is likely to be tired,
whatever her age. If she has a health problem, she'll find it
doubly difficult to cope. If Alejandra was anemic, that might
help explain the extreme messiness her mother described.
Treatment for such a physical disorder might be at least a partial
cure for the sloppiness.

Now that she's been out of her parents' home for nearly a year, Alejandra understands her mother's concern. She said recently, "We had problems with the housekeeping, too. When Eric would make a mess, I wouldn't pick it up right then, and my mother didn't like that. I wasn't a good housekeeper. I never cleaned up before I had Eric, and it was hard to change.

"I think teens should clean up when they're living with their parents, especially if they have a baby. My parents didn't ask for the baby to come."

Clean House Is Grandma's Security

Lorena and Doug Baird have a big home, and keeping their home neat is important to Lorena. This task became extremely frustrating when Melissa's boyfriend as well as their baby lived there. Lorena described the situation:

"It was horrible for me. I think a clean house is my security, and I had that taken away. At first I had a cleaning lady. She would come, I'd pay her fifty dollars, and in two days nothing was different than it had been. I told her not to come any more.

"I was doing all the washing for five people—it really got ugly. I washed every night and all day Saturday. Melissa had never done any laundry, and she didn't even know how many clothes she dirtied. The whole thing was overwhelming to her, and she didn't do it.

"Doug is supportive, and he was always talking about how neatness wasn't that important. We made it somehow, and we made it with all of us being friends. They finally moved out.

"Melissa and Blake came back a year later and stayed a few months until she and Pete got back together. That wasn't so bad because by then she'd had her own place, and she knew more about what it takes to keep a house nice. She picked up after Blake, and she did her own laundry. It wasn't the stress it had been before."

To Fight or Not to Fight?

Lois Gray is trying to avoid battling with her daughter over the neatness issue. She commented, "This housecleaning thing is never over. I'm either on her case hollering at her or sometimes

I can ignore it. It's my problem. It doesn't bother Robin, but it bothers me a lot.

"I'm improving. At first I didn't want those baby bottles on the counter, I didn't want the infant seat in my living room, but as time goes on, I've eased up, and the toys don't bother me like they used to.

"We redid a room for Robin and Roni when our son left a couple of months ago. When we finished and they moved into the room, we said, "Robin, we have redone this room. We've painted, and we've redecorated everything. We think it's your responsibility to keep the room neat.'

"For two weeks she did well. Every morning before she left, she picked things up and she made her bed. She's slacked off the past couple of weeks, but I've decided not to yell and scream and rave. Now I say, 'Would you mind finding a little time to pick up your room?'

"'But Mom, I don't have time.'

"I say, 'You can make time, and I really can't stand mess.'

"I'm trying hard not to have battles over the room."

New Home Is Too Small

Jessica and Lee Williams decided to sell their home and buy a smaller townhouse after their two daughters had moved out. Arlana was only sixteen, but she and her sister, Erin, had moved into an apartment and their parents didn't expect either of them to move back home.

Jessica and Lee had barely moved into their new house when they learned Arlana was pregnant and needed to come home. A few weeks later, Erin also moved home. Jessica and Lee's lovely new home was suddenly crowded. When Penny was born, the playpen, the swing, and the toys took over, according to Jessica.

At first, Jessica and Lee thought the best approach would be to help Arlana have her own space. This, they figured, would benefit everyone. Arlana and her baby would have privacy, and the lives of the rest of the family would not be so drastically changed. So they gave Arlana the bigger bedroom upstairs.

"We fixed it up with a crib, a TV, and a rocking chair, and we thought she would stay up there with the baby," Jessica recalled.

"We thought at first she would be with us no more than six weeks. Those six weeks stretched into two years, and early on, she brought the playpen downstairs, and the toys were everywhere. Arlana always wanted to be downstairs, always reminding us the baby was here. I'd walk into the family room, and there would be diapers everywhere. I resented it more and more.

"When Penny started crawling, we had to babyproof our home, and we hadn't planned to do that."

"Arlana's room was as much a disaster after she had the baby as it was before," Lee observed. "She was still the same teenager as she was before she gave birth. Her room continued to be a disaster. As much as possible, we ignored the room. Of course she wanted to eat in her room, she wanted to eat in the living room in front of the TV, and Penny would eat in there with her. The carpets were always dirty—they needed cleaning every two months instead of every year."

"The worst thing was when Arlana got pregnant, and the best thing that ever happened to me was Penny."

A year after Arlana and her daughter moved out, Jessica reflected, "I was in a class recently where someone asked us to name the best thing and the worst thing that had ever happened to us. I said the worst thing was when Arlana got pregnant, and the best thing that ever happened to me was Penny. I decided this after they moved out, probably not until they had been gone six months. That's when I finally turned into what I thought a grandmother could be. 'You can do anything you want while you're here. So what if you spill juice on the carpet? In two hours, you'll walk out the door, I'll clean my carpet, and it won't make any difference.'"

Moving into Partner's Home

Occasionally it's the grandparent who leaves the mess. Leslee Burnette was seventeen when she and one-month-old Jodee moved in with Jodee's father, Stan, and his mother. They lived with Stan's mother for two years, and Leslee had a different

problem. It was Leslee's mother-in-law who hated housework
and did as little as possible.

"I couldn't please her in any way, although now that we don't
live there, we get along great," Leslee observed. "I think it was
hard because Stan was her baby, and maybe she thought I was
trying to control things. I'd keep the house super clean—she's
messy—and she'd say it was too clean, so I'd lighten up. Then
she would say I wasn't doing my job.

"Her house was dirty, and she couldn't find anything. She'd
leave drawers open, and when I'd go by, I'd close them. Sometimes Jodee, who was two, would do the same thing.

"Just little things—like she liked her curtains shut, and it's
always dark in there. I didn't realize that, and I'd open them. I
needed to remember it was their house.

"Before I moved in, perhaps we could have agreed on what
would have been fair with the work around the house. Maybe
we could have shared—one day you clean the kitchen and
I'll cook."

Need for Advance Planning

Delores Holmes, Director of Our Place, looks at the problems
within most three-generation families and comments, "I don't
have a handle on how to solve it other than through communication before the baby gets here. If they are going to keep the
baby, they need to sit down and plan it out. They need to work it
out, and I don't think people do that. If they negotiate rules and
responsibilities, they will be on the road to coping with this
major change in their lives.

"What is this going to mean for everyone in terms of schedule changes, habits of the house, sleeping arrangements? All
these things will be changing with the baby's birth. Who is
willing to make these changes? What about the financial responsibility? Transportation? Everything changes with a new baby,
but families usually don't think about that.

"Grandparents need to make definite plans for enjoying some
peaceful time. That can be part of the negotiating process—that
there be a time when the girl and the baby are not in the house
so the grandmother will have some time to herself."

Working Out a Contract

Working out agreements with each family member as to who does which household tasks would be helpful for most families. In fact, an informal *written* contract developed *before* the baby is born could prevent some of the unpleasantness later.

The contract idea can be helpful in any family with adolescent sons and daughters. Negotiating rules concerning use of the car, vacuuming duty, cooking and dishwashing assignments, and other tasks can work toward everyone's advantage. Teenagers who feel they have some control over the situation tend to be more cooperative.

If the teenager has a baby, the situation is much more complicated. There is more work to do. Changes in the family cause added stress for everybody living in the home. While the young mother is expected to care for her child, her physical health may make this difficult during the first week or two after delivery.

Ideally, housekeeping tasks will be "contracted" *before* the baby is born. If family members already have some system for getting the house clean and the food prepared, it should be easy to adapt that plan to coping with the baby's arrival. Who cooks and who washes dishes? Will the young mother be excused from some of her regular duties when her baby is tiny and keeps her up at night?

Will the young mother continue to do her share of non-baby-related household tasks after her baby is born? Or will consideration be given to the additional work she will have as a parent? Someone needs to be responsible for such tasks as vacuuming, dusting, cooking, cleaning the kitchen, cleaning the bathrooms, and handling clutter in the family areas.

What is an acceptable compromise between your desire for a clean house and the disorderliness so hard to avoid when the household includes a baby—especially if that baby's mother is an adolescent with little previous commitment to neatness? Lee Williams commented earlier that having a baby didn't turn his daughter into a neat person. Her room continued to be the disaster area it had been throughout her adolescence.

Does each person take care of his/her room? Some parents are able to shut the door to their daughter's room and forget it—

but they may insist that she not be slovenly in the living areas of
their home.

Baby-related tasks are another matter. Will the young mother
always get up with her baby at night? Will she be expected to
take complete charge of her baby including picking up after the
baby, preparing the baby's food, and arranging for childcare
when necessary?

How will she dispose of baby's diapers? What is the routine
with empty nursing bottles? Toys? Who does the laundry? If she
is responsible for washing her own and her baby's things, does it
matter when she does so?

If the young mother rooms with her sister, and now baby
makes three, the sister needs to be brought into the negotiations.
Sis may basically resent having a baby in her room, and if this
means the room is in worse shape than ever, she may truly rebel.
Each family's contract should, of course, include all items
relevant to that family.

Siblings should be considered in any family contract. Will
they be expected to do some of their sister's household tasks if
the baby keeps her up at night? Siblings are likely to resent any
prolonged increase in their responsibilities due to their sister
having a child.

Settle Issues Before Baby Is Born

Before the baby is born is the time to formalize these agreements. Parents and daughter need to spell out the various
childcare tasks. How much will Mother and Dad get involved?
Even if the young mother expects to take full responsibility,
there will be times when her baby is sick and she needs assistance, or times when she is ill herself and finds it doubly
difficult to care for her baby. Will Mom pitch in?

Resentment surfaced again and again in these interviews as
parents talked about their frustrations with daughters who left
diapers and bottles in the living room and toys all over the
house. This is the kind of day to day resentment that can build
into much bigger problems than some teenagers can possibly
imagine. Working out an agreement before the baby's birth,
an agreement that parents and daughter work out and sign

144   Who Picks Up the Diapers?

Contract Issues

- **Housecleaning.** Include care of communal living area, bathroom(s), and individuals' rooms. Plan for handling baby clutter.
- **Meal Preparation and Cleanup.** Regular schedule plus anticipated changes after baby's birth.
- **Laundry.** Specify who does it, when, and how.
- **Childcare.** Who takes care of the baby?
- **Discipline.** Who's in charge? Working out disagreements.
- **Education.** Childcare and transportation. Help to be provided by grandparents and/or other family members.
- **Medical Coverage.** Health insurance or other arrangement for paying medical bills.
- **Financial.** Work plan for young parent(s). Responsibility for baby's expenses. Extent of assistance to be provided by grandparents.
- **Teen Parent's Social Activities.** Curfew. Contact with baby's father. Dating rules.
- **Car.** Extent of use by teen parent. Define who pays for gas, insurance and repairs.
- **Telephone.** Limits to use. Who pays?
- **Music/Television.** Define limits (if any) on volume, type of music or program, and timing.
- **Rights of Individuals.** Include grandparents, teen parent, other members of household.
- **Changing the Contract.** Procedure for contract changes.
- **Signature.** All household members.

---

together, may provide a push toward less frustration in this area for everyone.

How much are the grandparents willing to babysit? Are they to be always on call? How much advance notice do they need? Nearly every young mother I interviewed "knew someone" who expected her parents to take care of the baby whenever the young mother wanted to go out. Few of the families interviewed had agreed to this sort of arrangement (actually, lack of an arrangement). Instead, they needed to be asked, and they needed to feel free to say "No" if they wished, whether or not they were going to be home "with nothing else to do" at the requested time. Also important to these grandparents was the simple act of being thanked when they filled in as babysitters.

Is the young mother expected to continue in school? Who will take care of the baby while she's in class? Is she expected to attend classes regularly, missing only if she or her baby is ill? Does she have transportation to get herself to school and her baby to childcare? Will she attend summer school? Go on to college? If so, what help will she need from her parents? Or from the baby's father and/or his parents?

Is the young mother to get a job and pay her own and her baby's expenses? Or can she work off some expenses at home?

What about health insurance? Is there health insurance for mother and baby? Who is responsible for handling the paperwork? If there is no insurance, how will these expenses be paid?

Will she continue to abide by the same rules regarding curfew and other issues as she would if she were not a parent? Will dating rules remain the same as before pregnancy? Will the young father, if he is involved, be able to spend as much time as he likes with her and with his child?

"It's a strange relationship because we're still in control to some extent," mused Warren Boltz. "There are still rules here, even for her. Lupe's in the middle, trying to make rules for her son while she abides by the rules of the house."

Who's in charge of the childrearing? Do the grandparents set any limits as to whether or not the young mother will have complete control of her child? Ideally, the mother is in charge, but health and safety guidelines may be needed.

Who has the main responsibility for disciplining this child? Discipline during the early months generally refers to the need to respond to baby's cries as promptly as possible. When the baby becomes a toddler, the world changes. Grandparents and parent may have widely differing views on discipline.

Will there be limits on the use of the stereo and television— volume, type of music or program, and hours when they are played? The adolescent who used to practically drive you out of the house with her loud music may suddenly feel the need to have a quiet house so the baby can sleep.

If the teen parent has a car, who pays for the gas, insurance, and repairs? Will she be using the family car? For what purposes and when? If she doesn't yet have a driver's license, will she become licensed as soon as possible as a step toward independence? Or, as with many non-parenting teens, is her driving contingent upon good behavior?

What about telephone use? Who pays the bills? The cost of long-distance calls can mount up quickly, especially if her partner is out of town. Does she tend toward long phone conversations? If so, what will she do when the baby needs something and she's on the phone? Will "Get the baby, Mom. I'm on the phone" be acceptable?

The contract may include a section on the rights of grandparents and another on the rights of the teen parent(s). Can some degree of privacy for each, at least for limited amounts of time, be worked out? Is there space where each can retreat for occasional solitude? What other rights are important to each member of the family?

The teen parent, her parent(s), and other family members need to sign the contract. If the teen's partner is living with the family, he, of course, should be involved in working out the contract, and he would also sign it.

Your contract will probably need to be renegotiated frequently. How and when will this be done? Because of the multiple relationships involved in three-generation living, perhaps regularly scheduled family meetings would be helpful. Updating the contract could be discussed at any family member's request.

Planning ahead is essential for families facing the stress of three-generation living. Working out a contract covering each family member's rights and responsibilities can prevent some of the problems sure to arise when an adolescent parent, her child, and her parents live together. Hopefully, "who picks up the diapers" will not become a major problem for the family.

CHAPTER 9

Who Pays
The Bills?

Money? Oh God, it's awful. I don't have AFDC, and I only make $400 a month. I work four hours a day. I applied for welfare, but my mom and I are about ten dollars over the limit. My boyfriend helps out a little and I do what I can, but my mom takes care of most of it. Abby Peters, seventeen, mother of Latasha, eighteen months.

We had talked about early retirement, but the added financial responsibility of the baby means that's gone by the wayside. Toby Erickson, father of Jamie, pregnant at fifteen.

Babies Are Expensive

Money may not buy happiness, but the lack of it can cause a lot of misery. Adding a baby to the household is expensive, and for many families, these expenses mean hardship or, at the very least, a change in spending habits.

Many of the families talked about financial problems made worse because of the baby's expenses. Several mentioned early retirement plans which had to be put on hold for an indefinite period of time because of these unexpected expenses. Fathers who were finding it difficult to pay the bills for their growing families suddenly were faced with this baby who needed diapers, formula, clothes, and medical care.

Single-parent families are hit even harder with the financial burden of an extra child in the family. Mothers who were barely able to support their own children now have a grandchild to support. If the baby's mother continues her education, adequate childcare must be found. If Grandma is already working away from home, and if the teen mother's school offers no childcare help, the expense of hiring someone to care for the baby may be prohibitive.

Baby's Father's Role

The teen mother's parents are responsible for her support until she is eighteen, but legally, the baby's father is responsible for at least part of the child's financial support. In one state, if the father is younger than eighteen, *his* parents, along with the teen mother's parents, are responsible for the baby's support.

If the father denies paternity or if he has no job, or if the young mother refuses to pursue financial support from him, the baby's expenses will in reality become the responsibility of the teen mother and her family.

Even if the baby's father is involved, however, he may not have a job. Pete was seventeen and jobless when he and Melissa came back to her parents' house to live. Melissa's mother got Pete a job, and Pete stuck with it even though he hated the hard work.

Why didn't he take the easy way out and quit? Melissa's father, Doug, theorized, "We probably suggested by example even more than talk that there was no option. In this household, the only option is work. I don't remember putting this into words, but by our actions we communicated that we wouldn't tolerate anyone lying around and not working. It's not acceptable to do anything else. It's your problem, and you have to do something about it.

"For whatever reason, other than a few outbursts, he wasn't especially rebellious."

Martha and Brian Simpson found their son-in-law, David, was not so easily influenced. David doesn't work regularly, and the young couple receives some help from welfare. Martha and Brian have been very supportive, and have provided limited financial assistance. At the same time, they know how important it is for Amy and David to become self-sufficient.

Amy and David were married several months before their baby was born. Off and on, they have lived with David's parents, Amy's parents, and by themselves. David works part of the time, and part of the time he doesn't, which bothers Amy's parents a great deal. They discussed the situation:

Brian: "He's the youngest of six kids and has always been spoiled rotten. If he were working . . . if he made a strong effort to find work . . . he seems to have the ability, but he doesn't have the push."

Martha: "We can't provide the motivation. He should set his goals and pursue them. Sometimes we want to shake them both, but kids have to learn the hard way. Natural consequences can teach them more than we ever could."

Brian: "I think the first thing to do is decide who has the problem, you or the other person. If the other person does, then it's not your problem. And this is Amy's problem. I'm not being mean or nasty about it, but if we tried to solve every one of her problems, she wouldn't learn herself, and I think she has come a long way.

"We try to give the message that we're here to help, but we aren't going to support them.

"We don't just hand over money because I don't think that's the answer."

"If they didn't have food, we'd buy groceries and take them over there, but we don't want to give them a free ride. If he weren't able to hold a job, we'd feel more responsibility."

Martha: "We don't just hand over money because I don't think that's the answer. We get diapers for Erica occasionally.

I co-signed for Amy's car because there was no way in the world they'd have a safe car by themselves. That was a big thing we felt we had to do. We also took out a loan when she needed money for rent. She is never late with her payments for the loan.

"Amy and David are getting help from welfare. I have stressed to Amy that welfare is not a way of life, and I think she's hearing me."

Paying the Medical Bills

Families with no health insurance, whether for pregnancy-related expenses or for the baby, or both, face stiff sacrifices.

John and Nadine Adams had good health insurance for their own children but it did not cover a grandchild. They offered to adopt Marisa so she could be included in their insurance plan. They assured Colette they would "give Marisa back" later when Colette married. Not surprisingly, Colette refused to go along with this plan. "It would have saved us a lot of money, but we understand why she wouldn't agree," John observed.

Jamie Erickson's pregnancy expenses were not covered by either of her parents' health insurance, so she's responsible for paying her hospital bills. She explained, "I was working while I was pregnant and knew I'd go back to work after I delivered, and my parents knew that. I give them a check every month to pay for the hospital expenses. We went through a special program at one of the hospitals here, an adolescent pregnancy program, and they go on a sliding scale. Thank goodness my mom's insurance covers Dori now."

Juana Wolfe, nineteen, had to have a Cesarean delivery, and her baby, at four days of age, went back into the hospital for a week. Juana had no health insurance. "We felt it was up to her and the baby's father to pay these bills," Estella Wolfe explained. "The father hasn't been able to help much, and she's having to do most of it on her own. I feel badly about it, but it's her responsibility. It was her decision to have this baby."

Mom Pays the Bills

Maggie Hertzel, nineteen, had graduated from high school and was working when she became pregnant. She described the

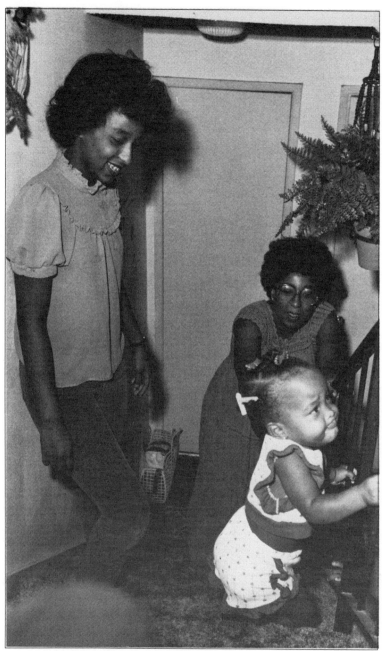

Who pays the bills?

changes this caused in her spending habits. "Before I had the baby, I had no responsibility. I bought a car so I had monthly payments plus insurance. I was living at home, and that was all I had to pay, so I blew money, paycheck to paycheck. I partied a lot and thoroughly enjoyed my life.

"When Tyson was born, I matured. I wanted to get my checking account in order, I wanted to start saving money, I wanted to become responsible. And I'm getting there."

Carole Fletcher also has a job. "I buy most of Kelli's baby food and diapers," she explained. "I get some help from WIC (Women, Infant and Children food program, Public Health Department). Usually it works out, but I have to budget my money real well. Sometimes I owe my parents a couple of bucks here and there, but they're pretty good about that. They don't make me pay rent as long as I do the housework.

"Kelli's father is still around. We broke up for awhile, but we're starting to date again. He gives me $20 a week for diapers which helps.

"I want to move out as soon as possible. My parents are kind of strict, and it's time for me to go. I'm trying to save some money so Kelli and I can move into a decent apartment. I have applied for subsidized housing. I don't think Mom wants me to move out, but Dad understands. Living here is like somebody standing over you telling you what to do and how to do it.

"I hope I can get into one of those subsidized apartments. I have some things I'll need, and my boyfriend is getting me a washer and dryer. I'm trying to get the necessities so that if there is an opening (for an apartment), Kelli and I can move out."

*The old idea of a hope chest
may make sense for teen mothers
still living at home with their parents.*

Carole is wise to be accumulating the things she will need when she moves into her own apartment. The old idea of a hope chest may make sense for teen mothers still living at home with their parents. Perhaps she can start accumulating dishes and kitchen utensils inexpensively at garage sales. If her family has storage room and she can afford it, she may want to acquire basic furniture items such as a bed, table, and chairs.

Doing this could accomplish two things. First, if an apartment she can afford becomes available, she will be more ready to move immediately. Second, the mere act of getting the things she'll need when she moves out will help her and other family members plan for her eventual independence rather than see her as being dependent on the family indefinitely. Psychologically, this can be a positive step for everyone.

Job Versus School

For some young mothers, holding a job and going to school in addition to parenting is too much. If she can, however, and she has childcare, it's probably healthy for her to know the realities of the financial responsibilities of parenting. Many young parents can't make that choice because they have no one to babysit while they go to school or work. This is a big reason so many teenage mothers rely on welfare for support. Providing childcare within the school system is perhaps the most important factor in making it possible for single-parent families to become self-sufficient.

If there is childcare available, but the young mother can't handle both school and work, it's important that she choose school. Without at least a high school diploma and job training, she won't be able to get a good enough job to support her child anyway. Surely the best possible use of welfare funds is to help young parents continue their education so they can become self-supporting citizens.

The same wisdom, of course, applies to teen fathers. They need their education and job skills in order to support a family adequately. Even if he wants to drop out of school and go to work immediately, this is not a smart decision. He, too, if possible, should find a part-time job in addition to attending school.

If Grandma Babysits

If the teen mom has no other source of childcare, should her mother quit her job and babysit?

If the teen's mother is a single parent and the sole support of her family, that choice wouldn't be possible. Lois Gray, however, worked only part-time. She decided to quit her job while Robin was pregnant, partly because she felt too stressed out to continue working, and partly because she knew Robin would need her to babysit while she worked. Lois had worked part-time, and her earnings were relatively small. However, her salary had gone for the new rug, the vacation, and other luxuries that are no longer possible for the family.

If this solution to childcare is considered, the needs of the teen's mother should be considered as well as those of the young mother and her baby. For some women, as is the case with Lois Gray, leaving a job she doesn't enjoy can be a positive step. Others, however, consider their jobs important parts of their lives. They don't want to give up the added income, and they enjoy their work.

Peggy Hanley, for example, commented that leaving home each day to go to work helped her cope with the stress she experienced as a grandparent-too-soon.

One grandmother, whose daughter was considering an adoption plan for her unborn child, offered to quit her job for one year and babysit while the daughter completed her final year of high school. At that point, she would return to work, and the daughter would need to get a job in order to pay her childcare expenses. The family was willing to make this sacrifice for one year only. However, her daughter carried out her adoption plan.

Career Plans Change

Colette Adams, although she definitely identified the father of her baby, chose not to ask him for child support. Nadine and John Adams assured Colette that they would support her financially until she could get a job and do it on her own. Colette was in tenth grade when she got pregnant. She was attending a private school which encouraged career planning. Colette liked little kids and had decided she would like to work in daycare. She didn't think she wanted to go to college for more than a year, and she thought that would give her the kind of training she needed to be a childcare aide.

After Marisa was born, however, Colette soon realized she couldn't earn enough money to support her child if she worked as a childcare aide. She gave up those plans and gained the secretarial skills she needed to work at a higher salary for a large aerospace company in her town.

Colette was able to return to her private school for her senior year because her parents bought her a car. She needed it to take Marisa to the Infant Center at the special school she attended as a junior. Colette's mother explained, "We believe that kids should pay for their own cars, but we bought one for Colette when she was sixteen, just before Marisa was born. The agreement was that when Colette started working, she could either buy this car from us, or if she didn't want this one, we'd take it back and sell it. She always paid for her own gas and insurance. She babysat to earn the money. If she wanted to drive, that was her responsibility.

"Later, after she graduated and started working, she paid us for the car."

Learning to Budget

A young parent needs to learn to budget her money. If Dad and Mother buy all the diapers and formula, she may not learn the financial realities of parenting. Non-parenting children and teenagers learn to manage money by having a limited amount of their own which must cover certain of their expenses. A young parent also needs to take as much responsibility as possible for making limited funds cover the baby's expenses.

Lupe Boltz, eighteen, mother of one-year-old Peter, has a job. However, she is still depending on her parents to pay her child's expenses. Her mother, Carman, reported that Lupe has been saving her money for a trip to California with a friend. Carman will care for Peter while Lupe is gone.

Being able to take a vacation is a nice luxury. In most families, however, the young parent will be able to become self-sufficient more quickly if, from the beginning, she shoulders as much as she possibly can of the financial burden of parenting.

Abby Peters, who speaks of her money problems at the beginning of this chapter, is learning about budgeting. She explained, "I get child support from my dad and that's our food money. I budget everything, and I make a menu for every week. I spend less at the supermarket when I do that."

The first step in budgeting is knowing what one is spending. How many diapers are needed each week and at what cost? Should cloth diapers be used because of the considerable savings involved? Does she know the various ways to buy formula, i.e., powdered versus liquid, and which kind is the least expensive? Some of this teaching needs to happen during pregnancy.

Heidi Winters, sixteen, started working when Danny was a month old. She attended school during the day and worked part-time at night until she finished high school. "All my money goes for Danny. I come last," she said. "When he was a baby, buying diapers and formula was expensive. Mom and Dad tried to help, but I wanted to do it on my own.

"I had a part-time job before I got pregnant, and I spent all my money on me. It was a big change to turn around and spend it all on the baby.

"At first I did OK, but after awhile I slacked off. A few times I went out and spent some money, then my mom and dad would help me. They would lecture me and I'd feel guilty, and then everything would be fine."

Babies cost money, and that cost is likely to add to the stress caused by unexpected teenage pregnancy—whether the family has a comfortable income or is dependent on welfare grants. The parents of the baby should take as much responsibility as possible for the support of their baby—although this frequently means delaying full-time work until they at least complete high school and develop job skills. Often it is the teen mother's family who bears the major responsibility for the baby's expenses. It is not an easy situation.

CHAPTER **10**

World Changes With a Toddler

I guess sometimes she felt like, "Will this woman ever get off my back?" The whole time she lived here she would say, "I'll be glad when I can get out and get my own place." And I'd say I would be, too. Alicia Martinez, mother of Alejandra, pregnant at fourteen.

When April started crawling, we had to put things up. Then when she started walking, she was constantly into absolutely everything. She still is, and it's frustrating. Belinda Hamlin, mother at fifteen.

Discipline was the hardest thing. Mom and Dad would say, "You'd better discipline that child or she'll run all over you." Then I'd sit her on the time-out chair and they would say, "Hasn't she been there long enough?" It was very difficult. Colette Adams, mother at sixteen.

Toddlers Equal Commotion

Most people love babies. They need a lot of care and sometimes they fuss, but generally they're pretty docile. The
caregiver feels totally needed.

Toddlers are different. They're little people with minds of
their own, individuals who still need lots of care but who are
finding their own identity as separate beings. A pregnant teenager may focus on the coming baby without giving much
thought to how she will manage when that infant turns into a
demanding two-year-old.

Judy Snook, Child Protective Social Services, Adams County,
Colorado, sees problems increasing for very young parents when
the child reaches the toddler stage. "When he's fifteen to twenty
months old and has reached the age of separation, the young
mother sometimes can't handle it," she said. "That's when I see
teens releasing for adoption—not a lot, but pronounced enough
for me to notice it. Last year, three of our clients released at this
stage. Either they relinquish, or sometimes we have to terminate
their parental rights."

The baby's grandparents may also find their lives more and
more disrupted as this child runs through the house like a
whirlwind, creating havoc as he goes.

Childproofing Helps

It is at this point that the needs of the grandparents—"It's my
house"—may seriously conflict with the needs of the daughter—
"It's my child." The grandparents feel they have a right to have
their house decorated in the way they want it, and they don't
want to babyproof all over again. Jessica Williams made this
perfectly clear when she said, "I didn't want to babytize my
house. I was through with all that."

Elena Stoltz, fifteen-year-old mother of Crystal, two months
old, is dreading this stage. "My mom is meticulous," she commented. "She likes to have her house real clean, so mostly
everything is in my room. Crystal's swing is in the family room.
But my mom gets upset if Crystal's bottles are out in the kitchen
or if her laundry is left in the dryer. Mom's a real nervous person, and it bothers her. I try to keep my room as neat as possible.

"I'm not looking forward to Crystal getting into things. My friend's baby is six months old, and he's starting to crawl. My parents used to watch him all the time while Shannon and I would go out. But now my mom is a nervous wreck when Shannon and her little boy come over because he pulls plants over on himself. He's always getting into something, and I'm not looking forward to that with Crystal. I know it's easier now than it will be later."

It is unrealistic to expect a toddler not to touch breakable items setting on the coffee table. If potted plants are within her reach, she, if she is a typically curious child, is likely to damage them. She may hurt herself, too, if a heavy plant topples over.

Childproofing during this time is likely to pay off for all family members. The child will be able to satisfy her curiosity as she actively explores without constantly being told "No." The young mother's relationship with her child and with her parents will undoubtedly be improved at the same time. The grandparents, while they may need to put away their treasured possessions temporarily, will also win because of these improved relationships.

If you find it difficult to consider childproofing
at this point in your life,
remember that this is not forever.

The young parent can be encouraged to do the actual childproofing under the supervision of her parents. Even if the family subscribes to the theory that a child should be taught not to touch grandma's things, (this may work with some children but certainly not with all), the safety of the child is of concern to everyone. Childproofing a house starts with safety. A good approach is for the young parent (and perhaps the grandparents) to get down on the child's level and look for potential hazards such as electric outlets, dishwashing detergent under the sink, and plants and other items that can be pulled over.

If you find it difficult to consider childproofing at this point in your life, remember that this is not forever. If you help your daughter work toward the independence she wants for herself

and her child, she and her child will be moving out eventually.
At any rate, the getting-into-everything stage will pass.

Paulette Barrow willingly babyproofed her house when Teri
started getting into things. Recently Paulette talked with a
mother who had just discovered her daughter was pregnant.
Paulette commented wryly, "She said if her daughter keeps the
baby, she will allow the baby only in two rooms. I told her I
didn't think that would work."

Respecting Others' Rights

Abby Peters, a senior in high school, has a part-time job she
loves. She says that's her time away from the rigors of parenting. Abby shared her philosophy on three-generation living as
she said, "If you have a baby, you need to raise it. I suppose if I
had a daughter who was spanking her baby all the time, I'd have
to say something. But I wouldn't raise it. When my mom doesn't
agree with me, she usually lets me alone. When she does give
me advice, I'll often take it unless I totally disagree with what
she says.

"You need to have respect for your parents when you live
with them. Respect their wishes. Some people say, 'Well, screw
you. I have a baby, and you can't tell me what to do.' That's
ridiculous. You have to respect each other even if sometimes you
have to put your foot down and do what you know is right.

"It's like with the baby. You have to respect her rights, too.
People tell me I should take Latasha out with me when I go out
at night, but I say I have too much respect for her to do that. I go
out after she's in bed, and I don't go out very often."

Abby's mother agrees with the need for schedules for babies.
She commented, "Latasha goes to bed at seven o'clock and
sleeps through the night plus she takes a nap. She's a good
sleeper.

"I'm a firm believer in babies thriving on schedules. It's
important not to take her out at night. If you keep disrupting
babies' schedules, they get all cranky and don't know what
comes next.

"Abby and I talked about this when she was pregnant. You set
your schedule around the baby because they need it and they

want it. Just like teenagers, they're screaming for limits even when they're acting their worst.

"Abby and I tried to figure out each other's territory from the beginning. You have to decide up front who will do what. Some of Abby's friends continue the life style they had before their babies were born, and the parents take care of the babies. We decided in the beginning, 'If you keep this child, I'll support you, but I won't raise her.'

"You have to set limits on how much you're going to do. If Abby says, 'Do you want to change Latasha's diaper?' I feel free to say 'No.' If she wants to go out at night and wants me to babysit, I feel free to say 'No.' Some of the girls at school whine because their parents don't help them more—and these are girls living at home and being supported by their parents. They still want to rely too much on their parents. They made the decision to have this baby and to keep it, so they can no longer be typical teenagers, going out partying and raising cain."

Abby and her mother are lucky that they agree on the need for Latasha to be on a schedule. Actually, the fact that they agree is probably even more important than whether the baby is tightly scheduled. Other families aren't so lucky.

When Generations Don't Agree

Jessica and Lee Williams didn't want to babysit until the wee hours of the morning, but neither did they want their tiny granddaughter out that late. They felt strongly that babies do better with routine. So they told Arlana they wouldn't babysit, thinking this would mean she would stay home with Penny. Instead, Arlana took ("dragged," according to her mother) Penny out often. Jessica was sure this would be self-limiting, that by the time Penny was six months old, she would complain vehemently at this disruption in her routine. Jessica hoped this would mean Arlana would stay home more. However, somewhat to Jessica's disappointment and to Arlana's delight, Penny adapted quite well to the lack of schedule.

Arlana also shared examples of her frustrations. "When Penny was six months old, they handed her a turkey leg bone to chew on. I didn't want her to have it, but I was overruled by everyone. I got really upset and threw a scene. That was the hardest part of living with my mom. If I said something, it didn't matter. It was a constant struggle over 'You shouldn't be doing this. You shouldn't be doing that.'

"Even today, I'm married and Penny is four, but it's the same thing. If I say no, Grandma says yes. I hate always being the ogre, and I feel she puts me in that position a lot. She was over here today with a box of jelly beans. Penny doesn't need sugar—that makes her hyper. We don't give her candy at all, and Mom knows that."

Junk Food Conflict

I'm amazed at how many teen mothers talk about Grandma giving the baby candy and other junk food against the young mother's wishes. They report that Grandma appears to feel candy is the language of love. "When I tell her my baby can't have candy, Mom says, 'Don't you love her?'" a young mother complained.

Babies and small children don't need extra sugar, and neither do the rest of us, for that matter. But babies are dependent on those around them for their life style, and their caregivers owe them the best possible start in life. Some families continue eating junk food but manage not to share it with the baby during that important first year or two. Others decide not to have soft drinks, chips, and other junk food around, knowing their child will develop much better on a diet of fruits and vegetables, breads and cereals, milk, and protein foods. Helping this child get a good start nutrition-wise is a wonderful gift from his/her family.

Sometimes it's the young mother who dishes out the junk food freely. Barbara Taylor complained, "My daughter gives Breanne cola instead of milk. I can hardly stand it. Breanne is only two, and Heather feeds her junk food all day long, and of course at mealtime, Breanne eats practically nothing. I've tried to talk with Heather, but she says Breanne is her baby and she'll feed her as she sees best.

"I agree that Heather needs to be in charge of Breanne, not us, but, while Breanne is a beautiful little girl, I think the sugar makes her hyper. At the same time, she seems to have less energy than a two-year-old should have. And she's sick quite often."

Changing Breanne's food habits now would be much more difficult than would have providing her with a nutritious diet from the beginning. And obviously, Heather is not going to listen to her mother.

What does Breanne's doctor think? Has he ever discussed nutrition with Heather? At the risk of being accused of interfering, Barbara might contact the doctor and express her concern. Possibly the doctor could discuss with Heather the importance of good eating habits the next time she takes Breanne in for health care.

Grandparents need to remember that children's appetites vary tremendously. Generally about the time of the first birthday, the baby will become less interested in eating. There's a simple reason—her rate of growth cuts back considerably at about that time. The typical child doesn't need as much food after age one as she did during her first year.

Another area of disagreement may be the appropriate time to start feeding solid food to the baby. Thirty years ago, the "experts" recommended feeding cereal to infants as young as six weeks. Today we know, through research, that giving a baby solid food too soon may cause her stomach to be upset because her digestive system isn't ready for solids yet. Feeding solids too soon may also cause allergies. Most babies do best on breast milk or formula alone until they're five or six months old.

When solid food is added to baby's diet, it should never be offered from a bottle. If baby is ready to eat solid food, she's ready to have it spoon-fed.

Too Many Disciplinarians

Consistent discipline is important to a child, and sometimes this doesn't even happen in a two-parent family living by themselves. If Grandma and Grandpa are also in the house, this often is a problem.

To spank or not to spank may be one of the biggest issues during this stage.

Javonna, sixteen when Justin was born, and Marcella Baxter
didn't agree on discipline. "Our major disagreement was
whether Justin knew what 'No' meant," Marcella commented.
"When he'd mess with the TV, I'd slap his hand and Javonna
would say, 'Don't hit him. He's too young to understand.'"

"And I didn't want to put him in a playpen and Mom went
out and bought one anyway," Javonna interjected.

"My husband drank more when Justin was a toddler, and that
made things more complicated," Marcella explained. "If Justin
was toddling around touching stuff, Troy would yell at him.
Then Justin would start screaming, and Javonna would yell at
Troy. It was a mess."

Colette Adams learned at school that hitting a child is not
good discipline. Nadine and John, her parents, didn't agree, but
they went along with Colette. John explained, "As time went on,
of course Marisa became very much like one of our children.
Although Colette took major responsibility, it was almost as
though there were three parents for awhile. I can't imagine
having a closer relationship with a child of my own. When she
was living here, we treated her the same as we did our daughters. If she needed discipline when her mother wasn't here, we
disciplined her. If Colette was here, we expected her to discipline Marisa. That wasn't always easy, especially when Colette's
ideas on discipline weren't the same as ours.

"At school the girls were taught never to spank, no corporal
punishment. I always felt that up to four years, a well-timed
swat didn't hurt any, but we had to respect Colette's wishes, and
most of the time we did. We used the time-out chair with the
little timer. When the bell rang, Marisa could get up. Until then,
she was to sit quietly. I guess this worked as well as the way I'd
have done it."

> *"They were her grandparents,
> and where should they draw the line?"*

Colette also discussed how her views on discipline differed
from her parents' beliefs. "Discipline was the hardest thing.
Mom and Dad would say, 'You'd better discipline that child or

she'll run all over you.' Then I'd sit her on the time-out chair and they'd say, 'Hasn't she been there long enough?' It was very difficult.

"They were her grandparents, and where should they draw the line? I introduced the time-out concept, and they were leery as to whether that would work. They thought spanking would be more effective, but they cooperated. Marisa had three disciplinarians instead of one, and for her, it was hard. She knew who her mother was, but Grandma and Grandpa had to have some authority, too."

Grandma Spoils Baby

Pati Adlof also says that disciplining her child is especially difficult because of her mother's reaction. "If I tell Dustin not to do something, Mom always babies him. She'll say, 'Come to Mama,' and I don't like that. I'm disciplining him and she's babying him. He goes right back and does it again. But I don't say anything because if I do, it's all over—and I have to live there now. When I get angry, I smack my lips so she can hear it, and I sit down. I'm sixteen now, and when I'm eighteen, I'm going."

Katie Rush, seventeen, complained, "My parents want me to discipline my baby (he's eighteen months old) by hitting him, and I don't want to do that. They hit their other kids, and they still don't listen. I want my baby to listen to me because he respects me, not because he's afraid of me."

Some of the disagreements between teen parents and their parents over childrearing techniques may be solved simply by a little compromise on both sides. The teen mother may be willing to respect her parents' wishes on some things if they generally respect her as the baby's parent and the one who usually makes the decisions and takes the responsibility for the baby. Her parents, in turn, need to think deeply about the relative importance of the various issues of childrearing about which they disagree with their daughter.

Some parenting techniques seem instinctual, at least for some people, but others can be learned. If the teen parent is taking a class in parenting, the grandparents might profit from learning along with her. Does she have a parenting textbook? Many

Teen mother bones up on parenting suggestions.

schools use *Teens Parenting: The Challenge of Babies and Toddlers* (Morning Glory Press) in their parenting classes. Whatever the text, perhaps the grandparents can borrow a copy to read. Teen parents and grandparents aren't starting at the same spot in this business of parenting, but they can at least acquire some of the same background knowledge.

Childrearing Views May Differ

While consideration of the child's emotional, psychological, and physical needs is of primary importance in all parenting issues, there are widely varying, but still appropriate, methods of dealing with these issues. We don't even have to look at different cultures to be aware of this truth. Compare the experts' ideas a generation or two ago in our culture versus their viewpoints today. When to start feeding solids, whether or not to pick up a crying baby, and many other questions dealing with childrearing had very different "answers" forty years ago as compared with today.

Grandparents and teen parents both need to remember more than one way of dealing with a child may be all right. Generally, consistency in childrearing is better for the child, and if the grandparents can respect the young parent's wishes in matters of discipline, feeding, sleep, etc., the child will probably be the winner.

Toilet training is one of these issues. In the 1920s, mothers were advised to start toilet training the child when he was three months old. The mother was to sit the baby on the potty on her lap. Washing diapers on the washboard made early toilet training important, even though it usually was mother, not baby, who was "trained."

Today we realize most children are not ready to use the toilet until well into their third year. Trying to hurry development of this skill is unwise.

In *Boomerang Kids* (Little, Brown and Company), authors Okomoto and Stegall suggest utilizing the concept of coaching in the three-generation family. The teen mother is the head coach who sets the rules pertaining to her child's meals, naps, bedtime, and discipline. The grandparents back up this system as assistant coaches. They agree to support the head coach in the system she designs.

Whether it's toilet training, eating habits, sleeping, or other childrearing issues, remember that it's the child who wins if Mother (and Father), Grandma and Grandpa agree most of the time. This requires adaptability on everyone's part.

TV Versus Reading

Another area of conflict may build around the television set. The television may appear to be a wonderful babysitter to a young mother needing some time to herself or to a grandmother exhausted from childcare. Statistics tell us that the average child spends more time watching TV during his growing up years than he spends at school.

TV addicts miss out on the active play children need for their physical development. Even a tiny baby needs to exercise on a blanket on the floor rather than sitting constantly in a swing staring at the television.

An active, curious toddler is often hard to live with. If the television keeps him quiet, it's a tempting out. But we're learning more and more about the adverse effects of television on children's development. Ideally, a child would probably spend no more than an hour or two in front of the television each day.

However, what about the rest of the family? If the television set in your house is on full-time, keeping a toddler busy doing more active things may be almost impossible. This might be a time to hold a family session to negotiate TV rights with some consideration being given to the development of this child.

When the TV is not on, baby is more likely to have someone willing to read to her. Children who perform best in school tend to be children who have had parents (and grandparents) who read to them a lot from infancy on.

Who's My Mother?

As Eric grew older, Alejandra felt her mother took over more and more. She said, "That's the main reason I moved out. Eric was three, and he wasn't really close to me. I love my mother a lot and I'm grateful for her help. I needed her financial support those first couple of years, but I wish she would have let me be the mother.

"The first month I would wake up with Eric and do everything. After awhile, though, my mother got totally attached to him, and she would wake up with him. A lot of times I was tired and I appreciated my mother's help but . . . everybody thought I was lucky because my mother did everything, but I don't feel that way.

"Even now when I'm living on my own, my mother pops up unannounced. I can't cope with going over to her house very often because Eric acts up around there, and sometimes he doesn't want to come home. Does this mean he wants to live there?"

Arlene and Jack Winters participated in the twice-monthly grandparent support group at Heidi's school. They feel the counseling there helped them set guidelines in the beginning. Arlene commented, "I made it clear right at the beginning that I didn't want to be a mother again. I had already raised my children.

> *"It's a fine line between the teenage rules*
> *and the mother rules."*

"We had basic house rules, but Heidi was also a mother, and this was her priority. Sometimes we would watch Danny, but Heidi was to be home before midnight because I can't sleep until she gets home. It's a fine line between the teenage rules and the mother rules.

"Heidi's mother instincts took over. She knew she couldn't run around, and she is a different person. She recognizes her responsibilities. A couple of Heidi's old friends came around after Danny was born, but they didn't have the same interests any more. Heidi said, 'They want to party and smoke pot, and I can't do that now.'"

Heidi, whose son, Danny, is almost five, feels her parents turned over the parenting responsibility to her. However, she, too, described the common problem. "He goes to Grandpa and he gives Danny whatever he wants. If I spank him, Dad picks him up and holds him. The counselor told them they needed to back down or Danny would be a little terror.

"I got terribly frustrated when Danny was two. At times I wanted to run and leave him behind, but I said to myself, 'This isn't going to last forever.' When Mom and Dad saw me getting frustrated or angry, they'd step in and take Danny or let me go out. I appreciated that."

> *"Communication doesn't just mean*
> *'I'll talk at you.'"*

Heidi's mother added, "In our support group we talk about how important it is to keep that line of communication open and have our daughter able to trust us. Let your daughter know you're there to listen. It's important for her to know that and not be afraid to talk to you. We don't have to agree with what she's saying, but we're to the point now where the shouting and the yelling has been over for years.

"Communication doesn't just mean 'I'll talk at you.' A lot of times we don't agree, but Heidi knows we're listening with open ears. That takes a lot of practice on our part. As parents, we've been right for so long. Our kids have to know we aren't always right. It helps build their trust when they know we make mistakes too."

Toddlers bring special challenges to the three-generation household. Good communication between the toddler's parent and his grandparents is more crucial than ever. Sensitivity to each person's needs is a big part of the secret of successful living for these families, sensitivity to and respect for the young parent, the child, and the grandparents.

CHAPTER 11

Helping
the Future Along

*The child must be the mother's responsibility. Grandparents
can get in a rut and take care of the baby, but you need to go on
with your lives. Don't have guilty feelings over it. I think this
helps the daughter grow up and become truly the parent.
Belinda still has some growing up to do, but she's getting there.*
Delores Hamlin, mother of Belinda, pregnant at fifteen.

*A lot of people thought I was going to give up when I got
pregnant, but I didn't. I still plan to go to college. You can go for
your dreams when you have a baby. It just takes a little longer.*
Belinda Hamlin, mother of April, seventeen months.

"I Thought My Life Was Over"
"I thought my life was over." It's a common refrain from
teenage mothers—and their parents. For many women, pregnant
before eighteen, life will be a series of hardships, a life of
poverty, of attempts to cope with too many children and too few

resources. But it doesn't have to be this way. Some teenage
mothers, while actively parenting their children, finish high
school, go on to college or job training, then get a job. They may
marry their child's father when the time seems right, or they may
marry someone else, or they may remain single.

The important fact is that teenage mothers can, of course,
lead happy, fulfilling lives, and many of the young women
portrayed in this book are well on the road to doing so.

Moving Toward Independence

Crucial to young parents' success is the support of their
parents at a time when these young people are not ready to
tackle complete independence. Also crucial to their success is
that this parental support be combined with a strong push toward
independence.

"Grandparents need to help their kids emancipate," said Judy
Snook, Child Protective Social Services, Adams County, Colorado. "One of the greatest gifts parents of a teen parent can give
is to push that teen parent toward independence. Help her start to
budget, learn to organize, and plan ahead."

Both parents and daughter need to learn as much as possible
about social services available for pregnant and parenting teens
in the community. Will AFDC (Aid to Families with Dependent
Children) be available if she keeps her baby?

What about subsidized housing? Section 8, a federally funded
program through HUD (Housing and Urban Development),
allows the Housing Authority to enter into a contract with the
landlord to offset part of the rent for the tenant. The tenant pays
a portion and the Housing Authority pays a portion.

Eligibility for Section 8 housing is based on family income
and composition. In many places, the waiting list is long, and
applications are taken only at specified times. Call the Housing
Department at your city hall and ask if they administer the
Section 8 applications.

"Grandparents tend to continue to think of that teen mother as
a child," Snook continued. "A complaint I hear often is 'My
mom still thinks I'm a kid, and here I am with a baby.' Basically,
they are kids having kids, but they need that little push to start

growing. They also need to have fun and go swing on the swings once in awhile because if they don't, they will be doing it down the road."

Juana Wolfe, nineteen, lived alone for three months, then returned home a month after Rickie was born. She wants to move out as soon as she can afford it, and her parents agree.

Juana commented, "Mom and Dad asked me where I planned to live. Did I plan to stay here forever? I told them no, I wanted to become independent. I want to move out. My cousin wants me to join her, and perhaps I can by the end of summer. First I have to save some money.

"I always have a hard time if my parents tell me what to do. I tell them, 'I'm grown, and I want to make my own decisions. If I fail, I'll get back up.' I know they're trying to help me not make mistakes, but I have to make my own mistakes. They don't want me to get hurt, but at the same time, they have to let me do what I need to do.

"I can't do what I want here. After living on my own and having my freedom, having no one ask me where I was and who I was with, now sometimes I feel like I'm still in high school. I go into moods where I think, 'I gotta get out, I gotta get out.'"

Juana's parents, Estella and Kevin, don't feel they interfere. Quite the opposite, according to Kevin, who said, "Estella does the baby's washing, and she does Juana's washing, too. I don't get on Juana's case. I'm waiting for my wife to do that, but she doesn't.

"My advice to anybody is to set up some rules in the beginning. At first, Estella thought she should help out because Juana was getting up at night with the baby, then going to work all day. But we need to talk about it because now the baby sleeps through the night.

"Juana is working hard to get her bills paid. The father of the baby hasn't given her much at all, and she owes us money."

Parenthood Plus Teen Life

Snook believes teens can combine motherhood and teenage life. "They can't have it all, but they can finish high school, they can go to the prom," she commented.

Teen parents, like the rest of us, need to have a balance in their lives. Snook describes this concept to teens and their families as a continuum. "If you're in the middle, you're on that balance. If you're too close to either end, you're heading for trouble. I think grandparents can facilitate a lot of that by allowing the mother to have her own identity and her own parenting style."

"Amy never had a chance to be a kid."

Martha and Brian Simpson worry that Amy, married at seventeen to David, had to grow up too fast. According to Martha, "Amy never had a chance to be a kid. You lose your friends. You lose a lot because people who are still footloose and fancy free don't want to be tied down. They call or visit her from time to time, but they don't have the same interests. I feel bad that she missed that, the growing up and going out and looking forward to doing things."

Alejandra echoes some of Amy's mother's sentiments when she says, "I feel like I grew up pretty fast. I want to be a kid again. When I go to college, I see all these college kids having fun, and I have all these responsibilities.

"I thought I could go out and get pregnant and take the responsibility, but with no money. As it turned out, my parents helped me get through high school. I didn't have to worry about feeding my daughter. I could concentrate on school—I had no excuse.

"It would be nice to be free for a little while."

Jamie's mother, Monica Erickson, talked about their efforts at helping Jamie become independent and about coping with the special needs of a parenting daughter:

"The biggest thing is communication—and consideration for everybody who's living in the house," she observed. "One of the things I want to know is that what I've done and the changes I've made in my life are appreciated, and Jamie is good about that. She'll say, 'Thanks for watching the baby,' and that means a lot.

"My goal is helping Jamie work toward independence, and I think that requires as much energy on my part as it does from Jamie. I think that's helping me get through this part of it. For example, Jamie didn't have a driver's license when she was pregnant which meant one of us took her to each doctor's appointment and other places. Now she has a driver's permit, and we're teaching her to drive. I'm looking forward to getting her to that stage of independence so I can say to her, 'I'm not going to babysit on this day and this day, and you'll have to take Dori to a babysitter.'

"Looking forward to her becoming independent helps me not feel so trapped."

Push School, Job Skills

Bonnie Slater's first thought when she learned Stacy, sixteen, was pregnant, was, "She's not going to graduate. How will she finish school?" But Stacy already knew about the Teen Mother Program in her school district and assured her mother that finishing high school would not be a problem, and it wasn't.

Stacy and I visited recently, ten years after her first pregnancy. It was raining hard that afternoon, and Stacy's four children were tearing wildly through the house. Stacy watched them calmly and fondly as we talked. She's been married seven years, and her husband has adopted her first son.

Stacy lived at home for three years, and she recalled those years of living with her parents. "During my last semester of high school, I took classes at our community college and got certified as a ward clerk, then started working that fall at the hospital. My mom encouraged me to do that. She didn't want me to sit around and not do anything. She didn't want me to go on welfare. She was afraid I'd get stuck there, so I worked for eight years after that. I finally quit, and now I think I work harder at home!"

Jamie Erickson is still in high school. She said, "I'd like to graduate, and I might go on to college. For now, though, my goal is to get out of high school. When I was pregnant, I said to myself, 'You can't give up your high school education, because without it, you won't be much good as a parent.'

"I can't imagine not having daycare at school. All the teachers at the Teen Mother Program are real supportive, and they understand if you're late with a paper because your baby was sick and kept you up all night."

*If there were no childcare at her school,
Abby says she would have dropped out.*

Abby Peters will graduate from high school this spring. She will work a year, then go on to college. If there were no childcare at her high school, she says she would have had to drop out of school. The college she will attend also has daycare. Abby's mother, Katheryn, commented, "The majority of the young mothers at my daughter's school probably won't make a big contribution to society—not because they have children, but because they already feel they can't do anything more than work at McDonald's.

"I have been blessed with a bright daughter who hasn't let her baby bring her down. She could have given up, but she didn't.

"As parents, we don't control our children's lives. All we can do is guide them, and when they fail is when they need us most. I don't understand parents who don't support their children in every way possible. They'll regret it because they won't know their grandchildren, and they'll lose the person they love most."

Lois Gray understands the importance of high self-esteem for her daughter, Robin, sixteen, mother of five-month-old Roni. "Robin doesn't want to be here for a long time," she observed. "Robin's goal is to go to school, get a good job, support and raise her child. She says, 'In a year, I'll have a house for Roni, and I'll be able to take care of her.'

"I don't see this as very realistic, but I think it's wonderful that she feels this way instead of assuming that Mom and Dad will take care of Roni forever. I think that's great.

"We have tried to bring up all our children to be responsible people. They have had jobs at an early age, and they were required to help around the house. Robin is working now while she's going to school. Robin won't have her house within the year, but I think she's showing a lot of responsibility for her actions. As long as she has some hope and some goals for herself, I don't look for her and Roni to be here forever."

Multi-Role of Teen Mother

It's wonderful and very necessary for young parents to continue their education, work toward their career goals, and have jobs. But what about that balancing act, of also playing the role of the teenager she still is?

The balancing act of being a parent and a teenager at the same time involves several factors. "Standard" teenage life includes spending time with friends and going to the prom, activities which will be cut back but hopefully not completely removed from the young mother's life. "Standard" teen life also includes school, and this becomes even more important for the young parent who will be supporting her child as soon as possible.

Attending school throughout pregnancy is essential. Young mothers who drop out during pregnancy are much less likely to continue their education later than are those who stay out only briefly after delivery. That month or two at home after her baby is born is an important bonding time for mother and baby. Ideally, a teenage mother will then be able to resume school attendance.

Robin Gray will graduate this spring when Roni is eight months old. Robin's father, Don, is strongly encouraging his daughter to enroll immediately in college this summer. Even if she takes only one class, he feels this will continue the pattern of school attendance. It's too easy for a young mother to fall into the trap of continuing her education "later."

School districts which do not provide childcare for students' babies are, of course, responsible to a great extent for the alarming dropout rate among young parents across the country.

Elena Stoltz, mother of two-month-old Crystal, says having Crystal only intensifies her career goals. "I have wanted to be a neonatal intensive care nurse for a couple of years," she said, "and now I'm sure I'll do that.

"At my school they will work with me to get a scholarship to college. I'll probably go to our community college for two years,

then on to State. I can't live off my parents forever. I have to
prove to them that I can make something of myself.

"I wish I could spend more time with Crystal. The next time
I have a baby, I'll be married, and I'll stay home a few years."

Is Marriage a Solution?

There was a time when the shotgun wedding was expected to
cure the problem of too-early pregnancy. Today, the publicity
surrounding teenage pregnancy often is tied to the fact that "they
don't get married." Less than forty percent of pregnant teens are
married by the time their babies are born.

But marriage is not a prescription which will cure the emotional, financial, and relational problems of too-early pregnancy.
Marriage is great—at the "right" time and between the "right"
people. If it's not the right time and/or not the right people, it
can be a disaster.

Melissa and Pete came back to live with Melissa's parents
five months before Blake was born. Both completed high school
and obtained jobs, and they stayed with Melissa's parents until
they were married two years later. They then moved into their
own apartment for a year, an apartment close to Melissa's
parents.

Melissa and Pete found new difficulties in living on their
own. Money was often a problem and, according to Pete, they
continued to spend far too much time with Melissa's parents.
After a year, Melissa and Blake moved back home, and Pete
stayed in the apartment. Pete commented, "We were too close.
We were with Melissa's parents almost every night. 'Come on
over for dinner,' and it was like we didn't have our own life. I
like Melissa's parents, but we couldn't grow into ourselves."

Melissa and Pete are going to give their marriage another try.
This time they won't live close to Melissa's parents. They're
buying a little house in a community two hours away.

Career Plus Marriage

Don Gray commented wistfully, "I kind of had hopes that
Robin and the boy would get married after they got out of high
school. I don't see that now . . . but Robin is an attractive girl.

There is nothing that says she can't meet a good boy some day and marry him."

This father echoes the sentiments of fathers all over the country, the wish to have their daughters happily married with the assumption that the husband will take care of them. When life works out this way for a young couple, fine. There certainly is nothing wrong with a young man supporting his wife and family. However, too many young women still translate this possibility into the idea that they don't need further education and job skills, and that concept can have tragic results.

Every young woman (and every young man) needs to have enough education and job skills to be self-sufficient. This is even more important if she (or he) has a child. If/when she marries, she will probably still need to work away from home. If she becomes part of the minority of women who stay home, her education and her job skills provide the best insurance plan available.

Walker Bradley said proudly that his daughter, Sarah, is back in school this spring preparing to earn her GED. She has also learned she qualifies for a grant to take the computer and secretarial classes she wants. Walker added, "This kid fell into a pocket, and she's coming out smelling like a rose. It's good, because God knows she and the baby need it. I tell her, 'Just don't fall for the first man who comes around. There will be a man out there who loves this baby like his own and who will love you. Don't be in a hurry. You'll find the right person. Just don't be in a hurry.'

"I have high hopes in the fact that my daughter is OK and I have a beautiful grandson. I love them both, and I wish them nothing but good."

Marge Bradley is finally feeling optimistic, too. "Josie is almost a year old, and I can remember thinking back when we first learned Sarah was pregnant," she commented. "With the baby due in two weeks, we thought we might not live through all this.

"My mind said we would, but that was hard to believe for awhile. When this happens, you don't realize there are still going to be days that are filled with joy.

"Now Josie is such a delightful child, such a happy child, and Sarah's a good mother. Sarah's grandmother said the other day, 'Babies are a blessing. While what happened to Sarah was horrible for all of us, having Josie is such a joy.'

"It's a long, hard road, and I know there will be times for a long while that it won't be easy. But it's working out amazingly well for us."

When the Grandchild Leaves

While three generations living together often creates hardship for everyone involved, having their daughter and grandchild move out is difficult for some grandparents to handle. They may be delighted their daughter is getting married, or simply moving out on her own. However, they may have become so attached to her child that they will find the situation extremely painful when both daughter and grandchild leave.

Colette Adams was married when Marisa was four. Until that time, mother and daughter lived with Colette's parents. Her mother, Nadine, commented, "There were some tough times

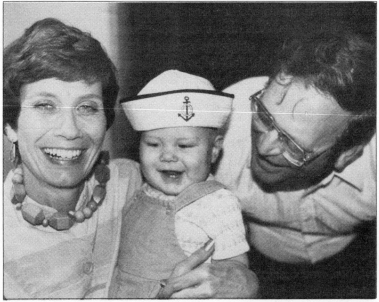

For some grandparents, it's a sad day when baby moves on.

when she lived here, but it was terribly difficult having Marisa leave. I think that was even harder for us than accepting Colette's pregnancy in the first place.

"When she's so close and you love her as one of your own children, and then she moves out, it's like taking one of your children away from you. When Marisa comes back here to visit, she's a fantastic joy.

"She lived here for four years, so a lot of home is still here, and she looks forward to coming back. But if Colette should ever leave her husband, I don't think we would open our doors to her. We'd help her, but it's important that she and Marisa have a life of their own.

"I do feel bad that I don't get my granddaughter very often. I suppose I shouldn't think this, but if I could have Marisa back by herself, I would take her in a minute.

"The idea of having two families living together has its tough times because we had no control. Having both a mother and a grandmother here was hard, but I'd like to have Marisa back if I could be in control."

Grandmother Controls Again

Kate Milton's daughter was three when Kate and Bill were married. Kate gave birth to Alexis just before she finished high school, and she began working for a local plumbing company a few months later. Kate shared her view of her mother's problem in letting go:

"The first two years were pretty smooth. I was working, and I had a babysitter. My parents babysat occasionally for me, but not often. They didn't give me a lot of advice, and they acted like they thought I was doing a good job with Alexis. But once I met my husband and we started going out more, my mom seemed to feel like she was losing control.

"So then my mom started to control more. She started telling me what to do. I don't think she realized what she was doing, but I could feel it.

"I had been working full time for more than two years, but when I was ready to move away, she acted as if they wanted us to stay with them. The transition was very hard.

"I'm a little rebellious, and I kind of broke away from my parents at that point. I know they didn't like that at all, but I had never had that control before. They had brought me up to be very independent, and now all at once when I was almost twenty, they wanted to take over.

"I thought, 'How can you do this now? I've been taking care of this baby, I've been working and supporting us, and now you're trying to tell me what to do.'

"I didn't take it very well, and there were hurt feelings. In fact, my husband and I moved in with each other before we got married because I had to get away. Mom and Dad didn't like that at all, and I think I did it partly to get back at them because they were trying to control me after all this time.

"Before this happened, I was close to my mom, and we could always talk about things, but this time it was my dad I could talk with. After I had moved out, he took me out to lunch, and we talked about it. I told him how I felt, and that I couldn't live with my mother any longer because she wanted to control everything I did. He tried to help me understand how she was feeling, and he tried to understand how I was feeling. After that, things seemed to smooth out. My mom backed off, and I know he went home and told her how I was feeling.

"Before my dad and I talked, they seemed to somehow resent my husband, but after that they've always accepted him. We all have a good relationship now."

Time to Move On

At what point should a young parent leave home?

When asked, "What would you change if you could start over?" Javonna Baxter replied, "Move out as soon as I could."

Javonna's mother agreed. She said, "As soon as I found out she was pregnant, I should have gotten her signed up for Section 8 subsidized housing. Of course welfare isn't enough to support her and Justin, but she could have gotten by until she graduated and could get a job. If you move in with somebody else, it usually doesn't work."

Javonna lived with her mother and stepfather for three years. Looking back, her mother, Marcella, advises: "Get them an apartment with their own stuff and their own access. Even if it's out in the garage, give them their own place and all the responsibility you can.

"It's easy to say now, but it wasn't easy then—don't bail them out of problems. Always be there for them, but make them take those responsibilities. It's too easy to say, 'You aren't doing this right,' and then do it for them, but they have to learn from their own mistakes."

Selena Slater is six years old. Her mother, eighteen when Selena was born, has a fairly good job, but doesn't feel she is ready to leave her parents' home. "I thought I'd be long gone by now," she said. "To me, living here is working out well. We do have a lot of problems, and there have been times when I seriously planned out my budget, hoping to move, but even though I make pretty good money, it just isn't enough.

"We're pretty crowded here, but my parents don't seem to mind. They have a lot of other grandchildren living near us. When they come over, it always seems to be Selena who gets into trouble—she lives here. That's when I'd like to go home!"

Danny Winters is almost five, and his mother, Heidi, is twenty. They're still living with Heidi's parents, but will be moving out soon. Heidi's mother described their situation.

Heidi was a quiet child, according to her mother. When she was almost sixteen, Heidi disappeared for six weeks. Her parents hadn't realized she was even involved with boys, but when she returned home, she was pregnant.

She was court-ordered to spend her pregnancy in a local program which included intensive family counseling along with its residence and school for pregnant and parenting teens. Heidi's mother commented. "Heidi never would talk much. Even today, when she's almost twenty-one, it's like pulling teeth to get her to say anything. Her school got us involved in counseling, and that was such a help to us.

"We knew we couldn't take over.
You're there as backup, but you don't
want to jump in and be in charge."

"My husband expected Heidi to place her baby for adoption, but she didn't. It was hard having her back here with a baby. We were there as backup, but she was the mother. Through the counseling, we learned to talk with each other. I knew I couldn't take over. Jack knew he couldn't take over. You're there as backup, but you don't want to jump in and be in charge.

"We watch Danny in the evenings while Heidi works. He's almost five, and it's time for them to move on. We're trying to help her become more financially established and move to an apartment with her sister."

The balancing act for teenage parents and their parents never ends. But if the roles are clear and the communication stays open, everyone involved—the young parent, the grandparents, and the child—will be able to go on to build satisfying lives for themselves. This can happen while they're living together as well as later when the young family becomes independent. For most families, this independence is the ultimate goal of three-generation living.

CHAPTER 12

A Therapist Looks
At Three Families

Twenty-eight families were interviewed extensively for this book. They are quoted throughout the preceding chapters.

The accounts of three of these families are presented in detail in this chapter. Each tells their story through the words of the family members. Following each family's vignette is a brief summary of the family's strengths and weaknesses from the viewpoint of Eugenie G. Wheeler, M.S.W., A.C.S.W., a licensed therapist. Wheeler concludes with an Afterword of her views on the school-age parent/grandparent phenomenon.

Wheeler has had a private practice for many years in Ventura, California. She is deeply involved in marriage and family counseling, and is an instructor at both University of California Extension and California Lutheran University.

Wheeler attended Columbia University, and completed her graduate studies at the University of Pennsylvania School of Social Work. She is the co-author of *Living Creatively with*

Chronic Illness: Developing Skills for Transcending the Loss, Pain and Frustration (1989: Pathfinder Publishing). She is also co-author of a handbook of marital therapy, and has been published in *McCalls, The Gerontologist,* and other publications.

The Morey Family

Shauna Morey and her mother, Nancy, are extremely attractive women who continue to live together four years after Shauna gave birth to Scott.

Shauna was doing well in eleventh grade when she met Darby at church camp. After two months of dating, he and his family moved out of state and Shauna never heard from him again. Soon after Darby left, however, Shauna realized she was pregnant.

She decided to continue her pregnancy and transfer to her school district's Teen Mother Program. She continued to do well academically and appeared to cope well with her dilemma. When Scott was born, his crib was ready in Shauna's room.

Shauna's mother had also had a baby before she married, and Shauna's older brother, Jimmy, still lived with them. His father had not been involved with Nancy since Jimmy was born. Two years after his birth, Nancy married Shauna's father, and they were divorced when Shauna was twelve. Shauna's father provided some child support, but that ended on Shauna's eighteenth birthday.

Nancy has managed to support her two children and Scott. As soon as Shauna graduated from high school, she got a job and began paying for most of Scott's expenses. She and her mother have never made any specific plans for sharing the household costs. In fact, they made no formal plans for life with a baby. They appear to have gone into it with an "Everything's gonna be OK" attitude.

Four years after Scott's birth, Shauna and Nancy talked about their current life style. As they talked, they seemed to be fairly agreeable, but their frustrations surfaced frequently:

Nancy: I also had a child when I wasn't married, and I lived with my mother. I had a lot of ground rules then, and I should have done the same for Shauna. That was my fault. If it were to happen all over again, I would change a lot of things after the baby was born. There should have been more of "This is what you're going to do." I should have said, "You're going to work full-time or, if you go to school, I'll help." Even now Shauna says, "I'll never pay you a cent for room and board."

Shauna: My brother never paid room and board until he was twenty-three, so why should I?

Nancy: You know that's because he was going to school. He started paying as soon as he was through. A lot of times you expect me to pay for everything.

Shauna: I don't ask you to pay for anything. I don't ask you for money.

Nancy: Think back to when Scott was young. He needed diapers . . .

Shauna: And I would pay for them.

Nancy: Not at first. There was food, there was medicine . . .

Shauna: You offered.

Nancy: I guess I thought it was my obligation to help, but parenting is an adult thing, and I should have put her on her own two feet. I was twenty-four when I had my baby, and my mom said immediately, "This is how much you're going to pay." I was lucky I had a place to live. In fact, I was real grateful.

Shauna: She uses Scott as a way to get me to do things. She says, "If you want me to watch him, you have to do this . . ."

Nancy: True. I wish I didn't have to . . . like picking up your own room.

Shauna: I know. It's not picked up every day.

Nancy: Why not?

Shauna: Every single Friday I totally clean the house.

Nancy: It is not. I can't stand anything left around. Towels thrown around, beds not made—it bugs me. It takes maybe three minutes to make a bed.

Shauna: It takes me longer.

Nancy: It's like trying to stop raising Scott, trying to stay out of it.

Shauna: Scott knows what he can get away with here. Scott knows that Grandma will rock him to sleep when he wants her

"Read me a story, Grandma."

to. It's gotten to the point now that I just let him go. Why fight it? He knows what he can do.

Nancy: I think you take advantage of me a lot. How many times have you left this house to go to a boyfriend's?

Shauna: I ask, and you say "Yes."

Nancy: If I say "No," you're mad at me. You huff and puff out of the house.

Shauna: If you're doing something, I understand. If you're just sitting here, I don't understand.

Nancy: I think you shouldn't just drop him. On the weekends you usually leave him with somebody.

Shauna: I do not.

Nancy: You walked out a week ago, and Scott said, "You don't want me any more, do you?" Sometimes I worry about him and the things he says.

Shauna: When Scott was real little, Mom didn't watch him as much as she does now. On my birthday she did the midnight feeding, and she would usually give Scott his bottle in the morning. That was her time with him—it just happened. We never talked about it. It just was done.

I never ever, even from day one, thought about adoption or abortion. You asked what I wanted to do, and I said, "Keep him," and that was it from then on.

Nancy: And we just made plans for the changes we needed in the bedroom, moved things around, and made ready for a baby.

Shauna: We have differences in discipline. You don't think I should spank him.

Nancy: It's because of the way you do it. You get mad. There's a lot you can do without spanking him.

Shauna: Mom paid for the hospital and for the diapers and the formula for awhile. Then she started asking me to do it.

Nancy: I think that in my generation you thought more—I wanted to make sure Jim was covered with medical insurance, and that I would be ready for emergencies. I don't think that part bothers Shauna.

Shauna: Not at all.

Nancy: It scares me. She did have AFDC, but they stopped it when she was making over $600 each month.

Shauna: I'd like to move out so I could do things my way, but it's no problem here. Scott has a terrible time going to bed, but when my mom isn't here, he goes to bed. We get along pretty good except when she starts talking to me about paying rent. I don't think that's fair.

Nancy: I have brought it up since you were eighteen . . .

Shauna: Do you want me to pay rent that bad?

Nancy: I guess I think it's the responsibility, and when you get into responsibility, you need to get your bills paid first before you do anything else.

All in all, it's been good. It's real hard pushing a child to grow up. I would change some things. Shauna finally started doing her own laundry last year. It's not a lot, but it's a help. Best thing I did about a year ago was put a laundry basket in there.

Shauna: You need to give and take. She thinks I take her for granted, but I don't. I know she gives up a lot and gives a lot, but I think I do, too. We have to understand each other. She has to understand where I'm coming from and I have to try to understand where she's coming from. She being older and me being young, I have different ideas about things—times change.

I do whatever she asks me to do, probably more than I would if I didn't have a child.

I kind of feel I had to grow up too fast although the only thing I really missed was going to the senior prom. I talk to a couple of my friends who are in college, and they're having so much fun. That's what was so fun about this weekend—to have fun by myself with my friends, and to think people do that all the time!

Comments from Eugenie Wheeler, A.C.S.W.

Shauna comes across to me as vacillating between abdicating her maternal role and wanting to take on the responsibility of motherhood. She says, "Why fight it?" (meaning why fight Nancy's taking over), then comments, "I'd like to move out so I could do things my way . . ."

Nancy does appear to take over, but how much is on her own initiative, we don't really know. We do know that Nancy resents Shauna for not doing what Nancy has taken over.

I see Nancy and Shauna going through the stresses of, respectively, too-early grandparenthood and too-early motherhood. Each feels so needy herself that it is difficult for her to see beyond her own conflict to be supportive of the other.

Nancy and Shauna seem to be ripe for some kind of family therapy. The goal would be for them to develop awareness of what premature mothering and premature and excessive expectations of grandmothering mean to them. Just the clarification and validation of their feelings would be therapeutic in itself.

Another goal would be to improve the communication between Nancy and Shauna. Short term communication training would provide them with the skills they need in order to be able to ask for what they want without accusation. For example, Nancy says, "You ask me to pay for everything," and Shauna replies, "I don't ask you to pay for anything." It is obvious that this combined interview has allowed both Nancy and Shauna to say things previously unspoken.

A third goal in therapy might be for them to develop a contract. Nancy almost asks for this kind of help when she says initially that when she was not married and lived with her mother, there were ground rules. A contract would only have value if it were part of a process which would involve their learning to ask for what they want of each other in non-destructive ways, then negotiate, and finally make compromises.

Issues that might lend themselves to this approach are the rent—to be paid or worked out; matters of discipline for Scott; laundry and other household tasks. The items would need to be renegotiated often, but such a contract would eventually replace the counselor and provide a viable tool in conflict resolution.

My impression is that Nancy, Shauna and Scott will muddle through—there is enough love, caring and limited insight. Counseling would probably help. The goals of treatment could be:

1. Clarification and validation of feelings

2. Communication training

3. Contracting

Such counseling would ease some of the conflict, clarify the issues, provide them with needed interpersonal skills, and help them to grow.

Teen Mother Living Independently

While the majority of families interviewed for this book were
intact two-parent families, eight were single-parent groups
headed by the mother of the teen mother. Because this book is
about coping in three-generation households, selection was
deliberately made almost entirely of families with the teen
mother still living with her parents and her baby.

Some of these parents didn't like the idea of adding a baby to
their mid-life household. All but one, however, managed to cope
with three-generation living for a period of time after their
grandchild was born. But what if the family can't cope with the
added stress of the baby in the household? What if the relationship between mother and daughter has a history of extreme
stress and the (grand)mother absolutely feels she cannot add her
daughter's baby to the live-in family?

Too often, this situation is "solved" by asking the young
parent to leave without offering her any kind of support. "You're
having this baby. You take care of it—but not in our house." The
result may be disastrous for mother and baby.

Is there a compromise? Is it possible to respect the grandparents' right not to have their grandchild living in their home,
and at the same time support the young mother in her life as a
parent but within a separate household?

Doreen McGee was as upset as many other parents when she
learned her daughter, Traci, was pregnant. They had not been
getting along well for several years, and Doreen was practically
counting the days until Traci would be out of high school and
ready to be independent.

The pregnancy complicated the situation even more. Traci
moved into a maternity home when she was four months pregnant, a maternity home which provided an excellent counseling
program for its young clients, and also offered a support group
for their parents.

Doreen attended the grandparent group throughout Traci's
pregnancy. Almost all the other parents in the support group
either had daughters making adoption plans or, if the daughter
parented, she and her baby would remain in the parent's home.
Doreen, however, with support from the group for her needs as

well as those of her daughter, decided allowing Traci and her baby to live at home would be good for no one.

She did, however, help her daughter find another place to live and assisted Traci in coping with living on her own. Doreen also agreed to provide extra help while Traci completed high school.

This family's experience, as related first by Doreen, and then by Traci, demonstrates another way to support one's daughter who is also a teenage mother.

The McGee Family

"Almost three years ago when Traci was barely sixteen, she became pregnant and moved into a maternity home. They had a good support system for her, and also counseling once a week or as needed for the parents. That helped a lot. I went every Tuesday, and they were there whenever I needed them.

"I had had a lot of problems with Traci before this—she always wanted to be very independent, and she started rebelling when she was thirteen. Her father and I are divorced, and for awhile, Traci and I were alone. Then this guy comes into my life, and there was a lot of conflict and tension among the three of us.

"This may have created some of the problems. My fiance wanted to be Traci's missing father, and she didn't want that. In the back of my mind I had thought, 'We're not going to make it. She's going to get pregnant.'

"But thinking this and finding out it really happened was different. When she told me, I sat down on the bed and sobbed and sobbed. I had a hard time dealing with it.

"She moved into the maternity home, and that didn't go well at first for Traci. It was a structured life, and she had trouble dealing with it. But she made a lot of friends, and now she tells me, 'Mom, I'm so glad you talked me into going there.' They were an unbelievable help, not only to her, but to me.

"While she was living there, I also had to come to terms with the fact a baby was coming. I had a hard enough time dealing with her getting big.

"Traci was hesitant all through the pregnancy. She didn't know whether to keep the baby or give it up. We talked about adoption during the nine months, and I talked about it on Tuesday nights at support group meetings. I knew deep in my heart that adoption was probably the best thing although my daughter never really talked about it that much. She focused more on the delivery, and kept asking what that would be like.

> *"All during the pregnancy I made it*
> *perfectly clear to Traci that,*
> *if she was going to keep the baby,*
> *she couldn't live at home."*

"Finally Traci gave birth, and that was without a doubt the most emotional time of my life. You have to understand that during the whole nine months I was trying to prepare myself step by step, first to see her getting big, then for the baby's arrival.

"All during the pregnancy I made it perfectly clear to Traci that, if she was going to keep the baby, she couldn't live at home. That was a hard thing to do, but I knew what she and I were like. Traci and I get along, I'd say, fifty/fifty. We're close, but my daughter is very domineering while I'm a worry person. We're constantly fighting.

"If she brought the baby home, I knew what was going to happen. I knew she would get aggravated and say, 'You and Quentin are home, and you aren't doing anything, and I want to go out.' I could see the baby crying, and she would be on the phone and expect me to change the baby.

"I worry enough now, and they aren't even living here. I know without a shadow of a doubt I would take over. I don't think that kid would know who her mother is.

"At the same time I would take over, I can see Quentin and me constantly fighting, Traci and me constantly fighting, and this poor kid in the middle. That's why I put my foot down, and she called me everything in the book, 'How can you do that?' And so on . . . during her pregnancy.

"After the baby was born, Traci wasn't sure about adoption, so she decided to put Tina into foster care. She went back to school, and she would take the bus to see Tina. Finally, after two or three weeks of this, she couldn't take it. She said, 'I'm keeping her.' At the same time, she knew she couldn't bring Tina home, and she didn't try to change that.

"Well, we had a lot of work to do, and I was willing to help her. We went through the whole system. She had to be emancipated so she could sign a lease for an apartment. We went through social services which was an ordeal in itself. We got food stamps and we worked out Section 8 housing. This all happened within six weeks, and the baby stayed in foster care during this time.

"Once this was done, we started to look for an apartment. That wasn't fun because most people won't take social services, and most people won't take Section 8. When Section 8 gave her a list of apartments, they tended to be in bad parts of town.

"I had already told Traci I would put up the first month's rent, and I went with her to look at apartments. I had a hard time with every apartment, and I started to have doubts that I was doing the right thing for my daughter, sending her out there on her own at sixteen with a baby.

"Traci finally found this apartment, and it was beautiful. The house was five years old, and the landlord lived upstairs. We had a couple of days to think about it.

"I was going nuts. I didn't know what I should do. I finally made up my mind—without telling my fiance—that she could live at home. I decided it didn't matter, although of course I hoped my fiance would understand.

"Well, I talked to my daughter and said I had changed my mind, that she could live at home. We talked about it, and Traci said, 'I want my apartment. I've been thinking about this, and I want the independence, and Mom, you're right. This wouldn't work out. We would be at each other's throats.'

"When I went home that night, it was like a fairy tale. My fiance, who had no idea this had happened, said, 'You know, if it's really bothering you, she can come home.' That helped me feel better about Traci actually leaving, the fact that we had given her a choice.

"That year was probably the worst I have ever gone through. Traci moved into her apartment in May, and that September she was a senior in high school. She had no way to get to school, so every morning I would go all the way across town to get her. We would go together to daycare, and then to her school, twenty miles out of my way. Then I would go to work. I was out of the house at 6:50, and driving until I had to be at work at 8:30. I was determined this kid would get a high school diploma.

"After Traci graduated from high school, her reliance on social services started to bother me, and I hoped she would do something, whether it was go on to college or whatever. She tried college for two months, then didn't go back any more.

"This second year has not been all that easy. Because she is a teenager and a mother at the same time, there are a lot of things I wish she would do that she's not doing.

"I also have trouble dealing with the fact that I never really got a chance to see my daughter go through the normal stages of life—go through school, graduate, go to college or get a job, *then* get married and have kids. I didn't get to experience that.

"I moved quickly from those rebellious years that were pure hell to realizing Traci was now my daughter the mother, the mother out on her own. She is only eighteen now, and this shows up in the raising of her daughter. Traci wants to go out and have a good time like any other eighteen-year-old. She takes Tina with her—she took her to basketball games when she was three months old, and I had a fit. 'How can you do this?' I'd ask. 'She needs a schedule. What about the noise?' We would fight over the phone when I'd hear about it.

"On the whole, it hasn't been easy. But then I wonder, what if she lived at home with me? I'm glad she's in her own apartment. I am. I do not regret now that she made the decision. I may not like some of the things she's doing, but on the whole, I look at Tina, and she's a healthy baby—she's a happy baby.

"I'm totally amazed with Tina. She's the joy of my life. I thoroughly enjoy this little girl. Even my daughter comments, 'To see you like this with Tina, it's such a relief to know you really love her, and that you're so happy with her.' There is a little bit of jealousy there, however. 'You seem to always ask about Tina, you seem to be always concerned about Tina. What about me?'"

Traci McGee's Side of the Story

"I felt real scared when I realized I was pregnant. My mom was upset. I tried to explain to her that I didn't 'let' it happen, it just happened. At four months Mom helped me get into the maternity home. I didn't like it at first because it was different from my house. My mom usually does everything I want her to. These people gave us a sense of responsibility, and I miss it now because it was the greatest thing that happened to me.

"I put Tina in foster care for three months because I couldn't make up my mind about adoption. My mom was behind me in whatever I did, except if I decided to keep her, Mom said I couldn't come home.

"Then when I found my apartment, she changed her mind and said I didn't have to move out after all. But I decided to take the apartment.

"I was scared the first night in my apartment, but I like living alone with Tina because it gives me freedom. I can't really come and go as I please because of Tina, but at home my phone calls could only be until ten, and now I can get them whenever I want.

"I finished school right on time. It was hard, but I was determined. Mom used to bring me to school every day. We had our arguments in the car because my mom was always picking at things I did with Tina, things she thought I did wrong. It bothered me because I knew I wasn't neglecting her. Mom would bug me that Tina didn't eat enough, for example.

"I have been staying home with Tina since I graduated. I started college, but I quit. I couldn't handle school, partly because I didn't have daycare for awhile. Now I have another job, door to door, but I make appointments.

"I want to go to at least two years of school, and I want a good job. I'm on social services (welfare) now, and I don't want to stay on that. They do a lot, but they don't give me enough money to spend. I need more.

"I didn't understand her not letting me stay home. But when I got the apartment, she decided I should come home. She still thinks I'm not capable of doing things, but I've been doing this for two years and it's not that hard.

"I have my family, I have a lot of friends, and they support me real well. I see my mother quite often, usually twice a week plus a lot on weekends. I still see the counselor at the maternity home, and she loves me.

"I think this has given me a sense of responsibility. I pay my cable TV and telephone bills. My telephone was cut off once, and that was awful. I paid it all back after they made a payment plan for me.

"My mom was worried about taking all the responsibility for Tina. I know my mom would have tried to take over. She tries now, and we don't even live together. I know Tina would have been calling her Mom instead of me. I like living alone.

"I know a lot of people who have babies who live with their mothers, and they never spend time with their babies. They are always out. Tina is almost always with me. She's at the grocery store, she's at the mall when I go shopping. The girls who live with their moms go out without their babies. I'm the one who feeds Tina and bathes her. I do her laundry.

"I feel like I missed some of my teenage years, although I wouldn't give Tina up for anything. But if I could do it over, I wouldn't have her right now. I know I don't give Tina the attention she needs all the time. I'm only eighteen years old, and I have my friends and boys, and it's real hard for me to think only of her. I need a life too.

"Doing things for myself is okay, but my baby needs me. I made this baby. I think about that all the time. I made her, she's my baby, and she needs me."

Comments from Eugenie Wheeler, A.C.S.W.

Most good counseling starts with helping the client become more aware of his or her options. It helps him/her feel less trapped.

In counseling families where a teenager is expecting a baby, the pros and cons of all continuing to live together, and the pros and cons of establishing a separate household for the mother and baby, sometimes need to be examined.

In Doreen's situation, it is understandable why she felt that she, Traci, the new baby, and Doreen's boyfriend, Quentin (who, after all, had no responsibility for Traci), "were not going to make it." There already was a lot of conflict and tension among the three of them. Quentin's efforts to be a father person to Traci had been rejected, so there was reason to believe that she would not accept any effort on his part to grandparent her child. Doreen was better at mothering and grandmothering when there was some distance.

Too much togetherness had a strong negative impact on the mother/daughter relationship. It is to the credit of both of them that they recognized that fact and tried a creative way to solve the problem instead of denying or letting it overwhelm them.

It is, of course, also understandable that Doreen would have some ambivalence about it, and vacillate in her decision that Traci would have to find other living quarters. In view of all Doreen put into helping Traci get to daycare and high school that first year, separate quarters certainly did not represent the easy way out. Just the best way in their particular situation.

We don't know much about Doreen's experience in counseling—just that she went to Tuesday night meetings of her support group during Traci's pregnancy. We do know that they both felt that Traci's stay in the maternity home was a positive experience and that Traci continued to receive counseling there. "I still see a counselor, and she loves me." That kind of validation eases the pain and helps to facilitate the many changes in living that take place in the life of a teenage mother and grandmother.

The Hertzel Family

The Hertzel family represents families who, with the help of a support group, work through their pain, their disappointment, and their anger at their daughter's pregnancy, and go on to positive planning with their daughter for life with baby.

Maggie was nineteen when she conceived. She was on the rebound from a boken engagement, and her baby's father wanted her to get an abortion. When Maggie refused, he made it clear he wanted nothing more to do with her or their child. Tyson is two now, and he and Maggie still live with Maggie's parents. Maggie's story is spread throughout this book, and her mother, Sylvia, shares her concerns here:

"I thought maybe Maggie was pregnant. I badgered her, I asked her if she had been to the doctor, did she think she was pregnant? I didn't want to believe my daughter was sexually active already.

"We're from a real strict Roman Catholic background, and I raised my kids that way. I ran the Sunday school program for nine years in our church. All my life I thought this was the worst thing that could happen to our family. We were the ideal family, husband, wife, and two lovely daughters.

"Maggie went to the doctor, then came home and said, 'I'm not pregnant.' We talked and talked, and there were some loopholes in her story. About 11 that night I said, 'Maggie, I don't understand some things about your story.'

"She fell to her knees and said, 'Mom, I'm pregnant, six weeks pregnant.' I thought I would die. It was awful. I just could not believe it. Even today I can hear it ringing in my ears.

"She says today I didn't even cry, but I guess I was too stunned. I remember grabbing her by the wrist and taking her into the bedroom and saying, 'You have to tell your father.' He was devastated. I don't know that any of us slept that night.

"The next morning I got up to go to work, and I was physically sick. I went to work because I never miss work, but my eyes were red-rimmed. I couldn't talk, and people would ask me what was the matter. I cried all day as I worked.

"We need help because we don't know what to do. My husband needs help because he feels awful, and my daughter needs help."

"I called Judy at BETA that same day. 'Hello, Judy, you don't know me, but I heard you speak at a mother-daughter banquet,' and then I broke down crying. I said, 'We need help because we don't know what to do. My husband needs help because he feels awful, and my daughter needs help.'

"My husband was heartbroken. All three of us went in and talked to Judy. She said things we didn't like, and she said things we did like. We went to see her every two weeks during the pregnancy, and I tell Judy we're where we are now because she taught us skills to cope. Judy says, 'Sylvia, you had a strong family, and I just prodded you along.'

"She really helped us. We have had a close family all along, but at that time Maggie was running amuck, going out and partying, on the rebound from a broken engagement.

"My husband felt totally betrayed. He felt that she was just . . . that the wool had been pulled over his eyes. And then Judy said, 'You know, your daughter's sex life is none of your business.'

"I thought, 'What the hell do you mean?'

"And she said, 'Well, your sex life is none of her business.'

"And I thought, 'You're right, but we'll have to deal with what's going on because of her mistake.'

"We went back every two weeks, and Maggie went every week to BETA for counseling. Judy made Maggie think about adoption. At first Maggie was going to have an abortion. Although she had written a wonderful paper against abortion in high school, when it got to her . . . she thought of it only to spare our feelings, and she couldn't do it.

"Here all my life I have preached, I have walked in picket lines in front of an abortion clinic, and now I had my chance to put my money where my mouth was, and I thought, 'If she got an abortion, no one would ever know.' And I thought, 'What a hypocrite I am.' Lots of people have had abortions, and there is no stigma on the outside because nobody knows.

"I said to Maggie, 'I hate abortion, it goes against everything I believe in, but if you want one, I will go with you.' It would break my heart, but I couldn't let her go by herself. I didn't want her to be alone. But she said no, she didn't want it, and I'm glad, but I would have gone with her.

"In the beginning, my husband thought adoption was the only way. BETA encourages their pregnant clients to consider adoption along with parenting. Maggie would tell Judy, 'I love this child,' and Judy would say, 'For God's sake, Maggie, you can love a puppy.' Maggie would come home so depressed.

"Judy made us think. She brought out to us that Jerry and I had no choice. It was not our decision. And you feel so stinkin' helpless.

"Maggie decided she would keep her child and continue to live in our home. We were going to be the grandparents, and she would be the mother. We wanted to establish this well, especially my husband. I'm not a laid back person at all, I'm a take charge person. He was afraid I would be the mother to Tyson, and our lives would be ruined. I would be the mother, and I would stay home with Tyson (which I didn't do with my own children—I have always worked). But the bottom line had to be that what Maggie says, goes.

> *"You have to be supportive,*
> *and you have to know when to shut your mouth."*

"That's my advice even if the daughter is younger. When they are fifteen, of course there are certain things they just aren't mature enough to handle, but the parenting of this child should be the young mother's responsibility. Now you have to help her out, but you have to put the responsibility where it belongs.

"I think the success of their parenting depends on the support they get from their parents. You have to be supportive, and you have to know when to shut your mouth.

"Then you must help them. In our grandparent support group we say, 'This is your daughter's decision, but you have to be the grandparent and allow her to be the parent, especially if they are going to live in your house. This is the only way it will work.'

"If there is going to be a parent/child relationship, the grandparent has to stand back and let it happen. We talked with Maggie about how she was going to be the parent. We set up guidelines before Tyson was born . . . we would babysit one night a week if she wanted to go to school, and one night a week if she wanted to go out.

"There are some things I don't agree with. We have had our arguments. We have our differences of opinion. About every three months we have to settle something.

"Before BETA we couldn't do that. Judy gave us these skills. We had a good relationship before, but I needed to learn to back off. That's my biggest problem . . . to learn to back off, not so much with Tyson, but with Maggie's personal life.

"When the daughter lives at BETA, her parents have to attend the meetings of our support group. Some people come to our meetings feeling so bitter. Sometimes Jerry will say, 'I couldn't stand to look at my daughter. I didn't want to talk to her.' When a man hears that coming from another man, and then they see where we are now, they know they can get over it.

"It's taken work, but I feel we're succeeding in our roles. This child has brought more happiness into our lives than we could ever have imagined. Because our daughter accepted her responsibilities as a mother, it has worked for us all."

Jerry Hertzel Comments

"We had to understand that we were the grandparents, and we weren't raising this child. If your daughter knows you're going to handle it, she may back right out of the responsibility. Even though you aren't going out tonight, you have a right to say, 'No, I can't babysit.' You can't make it real easy for her. She needs to make her plans ahead of time and work around yours. You don't have to work around hers. It's not your fault. You didn't give her permission to get pregnant.

"At our support group, we see other people who feel they have to watch their grandbabies every night so their daughter can go out and have a good time or work at McDonald's at minimum wage. We're pleased that Maggie wants to advance in her job so she can get out on her own.

"Maggie is a good mother. If she weren't a good mother, it would be different."

Maggie Hertzel Also Comments

"One of the best things we did was going to counseling. That brought us all together—a lot of crying, and I think that helped. My mom and I have said very unkind words to each other, but we talked it through. When the family can talk together, they'll probably make it."

Comments from Eugenie Wheeler, A.C.S.W.:

The Hertzels obviously have many strengths, not the least of which is the ability to make excellent use of counseling. That

takes motivation, willingness to look at one's own contribution
to the problem, a capacity for insight, and an ability to change.

Counseling or therapy cannot change reality, but it can help
change our perspective about it—from perceiving it as disastrous to perceiving it as challenging. It can help us recognize
options as to how we respond to a crisis—and sometimes our
response may be the only thing left that's under our control.

The Hertzels were open to learning ("Judy taught us skills to
cope. That has made our relationship with each other and with
our daughter so good.") After some initial resistance, they were
willing to accept new definitions of boundaries between them
and their daughter. ("Your daughter's sex life is none of your
business." "What the hell do you mean?")

They accept new ways of looking at the situation. ("Judy
made us think. She brought out to us that Jerry and I had no
choice. It was not our decision.")

> She was willing to learn to back off,
> to "keep her mouth shut,"
> and be supportive at the same time.

Sylvia showed insight into the kind of person she is when she
described herself as a "take charge person," and she knew her
limitations. Yet she was willing to learn to back off, to "keep her
mouth shut," and be supportive at the same time. This is a big
order, and part of her strength is in her willingness to accept
help in meeting the challenge.

Jerry speaks of how counseling helped them deal with
irrational guilt. ("It's not our fault. We didn't give her
permission to get pregnant.")

Both Sylvia and Jerry, with help, gained from expressing their
feelings, raising the level of their awareness of their feelings,
their needs, and also their rights. They demonstrated how they
improved their communication skills and established limits and
boundaries. Thus they became role models for other couples.

Would that more couples in a similar situation could be
exposed to and follow their example of courage and high level
problem solving. They are an inspiration.

Afterword

As I read this book about another dimension of teenage pregnancy—grandmothering—I am first struck with the tragic irony in our attitude toward the teenagers themselves. We give our adolescents so much freedom, financial support, time for fun, and so little opportunity to learn responsibility. Then, when they're in need, "in trouble," they suffer rejection at a time when they are physically and emotionally vulnerable.

While they are being deprived of normal adolescent gratifications, we not only tend to withdraw a lot of our support, we increase our expectations to a huge, unreasonable, and unrealistic extent. We insist that they bring their adolescence to an abrupt end, with little or no opportunity to rebel or to have any kind of sound transition from childhood to adulthood.

In our culture, adolescents go through a developmental phase when they have to assert their independence. Girls especially need to separate from their mothers, and for pregnant teenagers, this is difficult to accomplish.

So often people ask, "Why don't they use contraceptives?" Could it be that their conscious or unconscious desire to have a child is part of their trying to get out from under their mothers' domination? Are they attempting to separate in order to find their own identity apart from their mothers?

Some psychologists contend that the closer the mother/daughter bond, the harder the girl has to fight to separate. Perhaps it follows that this drastic measure (becoming pregnant) is sometimes taken by young women who are most dependent on their parents.

If so, the young woman's search for herself and her own identity is then compounded by the introduction of a new human being who, in a sense, belongs to both her and her parents. Does the baby then become the focus of the struggle, the dependence/independence struggle, that is a part of the girl's growing up?

It is true that we have come a long way. We don't stone women who become pregnant out of wedlock, or make them wear the letter "A" on their foreheads, or publish their names for listing in the town square. But if punishment means to afflict with pain, loss, or suffering for a crime or fault, pregnant teens and young, unmarried parents are still being subjected to punitive attitudes. Witness the self-righteousness in the old saying, "There are no illegitimate children, just illegitimate parents."

It is true that in our zeal to help young mothers become economically independent, we encourage these young women to go back to school. This is in contrast to the prevailing attitude in the fifties. Then, many school principals found all kinds of excuses to bar pregnant teenagers from returning to high school. They claimed that the baby would be neglected (even though a grandmother was assuming full care), or they suggested that pregnancy was "catching."

The stigma has lessened, but it is still out there. It's not only "out there" but also in our hearts, in the hearts of the teenage parents, and their parents, the grandparents. If a mere fraction of the emotional energy and political clout being spent on the abortion controversy were to be rechanneled to problem-solving in relation to teen parenthood, the next generation(s) would benefit enormously.

It is interesting that so many mothers are opting to parent their babies themselves in spite of all of these negative currents. It is also interesting that this trend is interpreted as healthy, or as unhealthy, depending upon one's orientation.

The parents of teenage parents are forced to examine their attitudes and take on new roles before they are ready. Often the grandmother was a teenage mom herself, and her daughter's pregnancy reactivates her own unresolved problems from that time. Although there are vast cultural differences in the levels of acceptance of teenage, unmarried pregnancy, it must come as a jolt to the self-image of almost any woman in her thirties to realize suddenly that she is about to become a grandmother. There haven't been the usual rites and rituals such as graduation, mother-of-the-bride experiences, and empty nest adjustments that constitute steps in a process that publicly and privately prepares one for a new role.

Before the usual mother/daughter tug of war related to the daughter's struggle to establish her own independent identity has been worked through, a new, highly charged issue is introduced. The grandmother may feel she has moved beyond mothering and finally gotten herself out of the home, perhaps with a job, or a new relationship. She may feel that her life is finally getting on track. And now her progression along the life cycle receives a blow and a set-back.

The usual adolescent issues of neatness, household chores, money, and value differences are suddenly compounded by an unexpected pregnancy for which no one is ready. The focus of the adolescent rebellion shifts to baby-related issues—the mother's care, or lack of care, of the baby.

Mother/daughter differences in ideal situations, we are told, are often resolved after a child is born. Mother and daughter now have something in common, and the daughter is finally willing to listen to her mother's advice. And she, the grandmother, shows new respect for her daughter as a woman, as an adult, and as the mother of her grandchild. Be that as it may, when expectations are suddenly totally out of sync with reality, the result can be everything from minor adjustments to be made to major traumas to overcome.

This represents a challenge to the grandmother. She is expected to take on a new role and responsibilities before she is ready, before she has survived adolescent rebellion and started to relate to her daughter on a woman-to-woman basis.

She is often called upon to be the buffer between her daughter and an angry, rejecting grandfather, to provide endless childcare, and to be strained financially. In addition, she must deal with the emotional stress of being unready for this stage of her life.

In writing about chronic illness, I learned that there is an inherent conflict between taking care of an ill person, and at the same time trying to let that person be autonomous. It seemed to me, as I read this book, that the young grandmothers were saying over and over again in many different ways that the effort to resolve this basic conflict within three-generation living is the most difficult task they have ever faced. They must maintain that balance between helping the mother with baby care, and yet insisting that the young mother take charge of her child. Such understandable ambivalence, resentment, and worry these grandparents must feel.

The individual ways of resolving this dilemma cover a wide spectrum. ("I think the hardest thing for the grandmother or grandparents to figure out is where they fit in. All of a sudden you aren't supposed to be a parent to this child who is now a mother. She still needs guidance, but you don't want to overstep your bounds and raise her child. And you aren't allowed to be a grandma, either, in your own home.")

Issues of control are the major focus of the mother/daughter struggle. And these control issues can include not only the physical care of the baby, but also matters of discipline, space, money, housework, etc. ("I know my mom would have tried to take over. She tries to now, and we don't live together.")

Some grandparents scapegoat the young father in order to avoid facing their daughter's responsibility for the situation. ("I stood up and shook a finger in his face . . . I should have been shaking my finger at her, too.")

It is easy to understand why the grandparents' marital relationships are often strained. They are ready for their children to leave, and here they are with a whole new family to think about, live with, and support in all sorts of ways.

Siblings, too, play a significant part in this new family constellation. In fact, the complexity of some of these families would be a family counselor's nightmare if s/he tried to do sociograms. The grandmother is often the mediator among all elements: *her* parents, the boy's parents, her children, her own partner (who may or may not be the young mother's father), school personnel, cousins, and friends.

Yet with all these stresses and complications, some grandparents come to terms with the reality in ways that inspire admiration. A grandmother may sense the need to mother her daughter, who, after all, is still a child, so that the daughter will be empowered to mother the baby. To quote one of these exceptional grandmothers, "I wouldn't say it's easy, but I would say it is the biggest joy of my whole life . . . If people would just let it be a joy . . . instead of moralizing about situations . . . I don't understand the turning off of love when someone does something that doesn't please you . . . I get very frustrated at conditional love. This isn't right. You wouldn't want that from your own parents . . . No one can live up to everybody's expectations . . . We set the standards for our children, and when they don't live up to it, we say, 'Goodbye.'"

Let's, as a society, stop saying "Goodbye." Thank you, grandmother, for setting a good example of someone who has thought through, and acted on, her philosophy, who didn't stay stuck in the futility of assigning blame, but rather learned to forgive— herself as well as the parents of her grandchild. And thank you, Jeanne Lindsay, for writing this illuminating book.

Eugenie G. Wheeler, A.C.S.W.
Co-Author of Living Creatively with Chronic Illness:
 Developing Skills for Transcending the Loss, Pain and
 Frustration

Three-generation living usually means more attention for the child.

Appendix

About
The Author

Jeanne Warren Lindsay, M.A., C.H.E., developed and for sixteen years coordinated the Teen Mother Program, an alternative offered to pregnant and parenting students in the ABC Unified School District, Cerritos, California. This program is a choice offered to pregnant and parenting students who do not wish to attend the comprehensive high school throughout pregnancy. Ms. Lindsay has counseled hundreds of pregnant teenagers. Many of these young women are rearing their children themselves while others have made and carried out adoption plans for their babies.

Ms. Lindsay has advanced degrees in home economics and anthropology. She has edited the *NOAPP Network,* quarterly newsletter of the National Organization on Adolescent Pregnancy and Parenting, since 1985. She frequently gives presentations across the country on the culture of school-age parents, teenage marriage, educating pregnant and parenting teens, and other topics.

Ms. Lindsay is the author or co-author of ten other books on adolescent pregnancy and parenting, teenage marriage, and adoption from the birthfamily's perspective. Titles include *Teens Parenting: The Challenge of Babies and Toddlers; Pregnant Too Soon: Adoption Is an Option; Do I Have a Daddy? A Book About a Single-Parent Child; Teen Pregnancy Challenge, Book One: Strategies for Change; Teen Pregnancy Challenge, Book Two: Programs for Kids; Parents, Pregnant Teens and the Adoption Option: Help for Families,* and four others.

Jeanne and Bob have been married thirty-nine years. They have five grown children and four gorgeous grandchildren.

Annotated
Bibliography

Not a great deal has been written especially for the parents of pregnant and parenting teenagers. Included in the following resources are a few such books, but the majority of these titles are designed for pregnant and parenting adolescents.

About a quarter of these books are geared to the needs of professionals working with this population. However, these particular titles were selected because of their possible interest to grandparents, i.e., they focus on school services for teen parents and their babies or present other general information on the subject.

Many of the books written for teens would also be of interest to their parents.

Prices, when given, are from the 1989 edition of *Books in Print*. If you order a book directly from the publisher, check first with your public library or a bookstore to learn current prices. Then add $2.00 for shipping.

Barr, Linda, and Catherine Monserrat. *Teenage Pregnancy: A New Beginning.* Revised 1988. 100 pp. New Futures, Inc., 5400 Cutler NE, Albuquerque, NM 87110. Also available from Morning Glory Press, 6595 San Haroldo Way, Buena Park, CA 90620. Illustrated. Spiral, $10. Quantity discount.
Written specifically for pregnant teens. Topics include prenatal health care, nutrition during pregnancy, fetal development, preparation for labor and delivery, decision-making, emotional effects of adolescent pregnancy, and others.

_____. *Working with Childbearing Adolescents: A Guide for Use with Teenage Pregnancy, A New Beginning.* Revised 1986. New Futures Inc. Also available from Morning Glory Press. Illustrated. Spiral, $12.95.
Adolescent development and sexuality are explored. Authors include their experiences, ideas, and insights gained through working with pregnant adolescents.

Becker, Kayla M., with Connie K. Heckert. *To Keera with Love.* 1987. 170 pp. Sheed and Ward, Kansas City, MO. Paper, $8.95. Also available from Morning Glory Press.
Dramatic true story of Kayla's journey from a protected, happy childhood to the harsh reality of becoming a mother too soon, and through her grieving as she places her beloved Keera for adoption.

Brindis, Claire, and Rita Jeremy. *Adolescent Pregnancy and Parenting in California: A Strategic Plan for Action.* 1988. 210 pp. California Medical Association/California Adolescent Pregnancy Conference, Pat Murray, Box 7690, San Francisco, CA 94120-7690. $20.
Includes a great deal of information which would be helpful to other states interested in developing a statewide plan for action toward dealing with teen pregnancy and parenting.

Brinkley, Ginny, and Sherry Sampson. *Young and Pregnant—A Book for You.* 1989. 73 pp. Pink Inc! 8230-1 Baycenter Road, Jacksonville, FL 32256. $3.95.
Refreshingly simple little book on prenatal care directed to teenagers. Provides basic information.

Brown, Jane, Ed. *Daddy, I'm Pregnant.* 1988. Multnomah Press, School of the Bible, 10209 SE Div. St., Portland, OR 97266. $6.95.

A minister/father's journal of his feelings and experiences during the pregnancy of his fourteen-year-old daughter.

Brownley, Margaret. **"A Parent's Guide to Teenage Pregnancy."** 1988. 36 pp. Community Intervention, Inc., 529 South Seventh Street, Suite 570, Minneapolis, MN 55415. $3.95.
Little booklet provides guidelines for parents whose daughter is pregnant.

Cahill, Michele, J. Lynne White, David Lowe, and Lauren E. Jacobs. *In School Together: School-based Child Care Serving Student Mothers.* 1987. 135 pp. School Services Division, Academy for Educational Development, 680 Fifth Ave., New York, NY 10019. $15. Also available from Morning Glory Press.
Practical how-to guide for creating school-based childcare centers for students' children. Covers all phases of program development.

Cassell, Carol, Ph.D. *Straight from the Heart: How to Talk to Your Teenagers About Love and Sex.* 1987. 255 pp. Simon and Schuster, New York. $15.95. 1988. Paper, $6.95.
Excellent guide for parents and for anyone else who talks with kids about issues related to sex.

Compton, Nancy, Mara Duncan, and Jack Hruska. *How Schools Can Combat Student Pregnancy.* 1987. 184 pp. NEA Professional Library, P.O. Box 509, West Haven, CT 06516. $10.95.
Excellent discussion of the school's role in teenage pregnancy prevention and care—an in-depth discussion of how schools can make a difference in young people's lives by dealing with these issues rather than pretending the problems don't exist.

Dacy, Matt, et al. *Teen Pregnancy* (Helping Others in Crisis Series). 1989. 112 pp. David C. Cook Publishing, 850 N. Grove Avenue, Elgin, IL 60120. $6.95.
A pro-life approach offering guidance to Christians who wonder how to help a pregnant teen and her family.

Emmens, Carol. *The Abortion Controversy.* 1987. 137 pp. Julian Messner, Simon & Schuster, Inc., Simon & Schuster Building, Rockefeller Center, 1230 Avenue of the Americas, New York, NY 10020. $5.95.

Recommended for anyone wanting to be well-informed about both pro-choice and pro-life viewpoints on this issue.

Ewy, Donna and Rodger. ***Teen Pregnancy: The Challenges We Faced, The Choices We Made.*** 1985. 188 pp. Pruett Publishing Company, Boulder, CO. $14.95. New American Library. Paper, $3.95.
A refreshingly practical guide for teenagers facing the hard choices and special challenges of pregnancy in the teen years. Good advice is coupled with quotes from pregnant and parenting teenagers.

Foster, Sallie. ***The One Girl in Ten: A Self Portrait of the Teenage Mother.*** 1988. 160 pp. Child Welfare League of America, 440 First Street N.W., Suite 310, Washington, DC 20001-2085. $10.95.
The author taped interviews with 126 young mothers. With their words, she offers a broad picture of the world of teen parenthood.

Francis, Judith, and Fern Marx. ***Learning Together: A National Directory of Teen Parenting and Child Care Programs.*** 1989. 220 pp. Publications Dept., Wellesley College Center for Research on Women, Wellesley College, Wellesley, MA 02181. $20.
Profiles three hundred programs serving teen parents and their children. Illustrates range of services needed by young families.

Gardner, Jay. ***A Difficult Decision: A Compassionate Book About Abortion.*** 1986. 118 pp. The Crossing Press, 22-D Roache Road, P.O. Box 1048, Freedom, CA 95019. $6.95.
Offers options and support needed to help women and couples facing unexpected pregnancy make a choice they can handle. Support is given for either continuing the pregnancy or having an abortion.

Hansen, Caryl. ***Your Choice: A Young Woman's Guide to Making Decisions About Unmarried Pregnancy.*** 1980. Paper. Avon. $2.25.
A comprehensive guide to the options open to pregnant teenagers. The author emphasizes the need for choosing an option rather than going into motherhood without making a decision.

"Inside My Mom." Sound filmstrip. March of Dimes Birth Defects Foundation, 1275 Mamaroneck Avenue, White Plains, NY 10605. $10. Also available from most local chapters of March of Dimes.
Excellent filmstrip on prenatal nutrition features a cartoon fetus.

Lindsay, Jeanne Warren. ***Do I Have a Daddy? A Story About a Single-Parent Child.*** Rev. 1990. 46 pp. Morning Glory Press, 6595 San Haroldo Way, Buena Park, CA 90620. Cloth, $13.95; paper, $5.95.
A picture/story book in which a single mother explains to her son that his daddy left soon after he was born. It contains a twelve-page section of suggestions for single parents.

_____. ***Open Adoption: A Caring Option.*** 1987. 256 pp. Photos. Morning Glory Press. Hardcover, $15.95; paper, $9.95.
A fascinating and sensitive account of the new world of adoption where birthparents choose their child's adoptive parents and may remain in contact with their child's new family.

_____. ***Parents, Pregnant Teens and the Adoption Option: Help for Families.*** 1989. 208 pp. Morning Glory Press. Paper, $8.95.
Guidance for parents of pregnant teenagers. Offers practical suggestions for providing support while encouraging the young person to take responsibility for her decisions.

_____. ***Teenage Marriage: Coping with Reality.*** 1988. 208 pp. Photos. Morning Glory Press. Hardcover, $15.95; paper, $9.95. Teacher's guide, $5.95. Student study guide, $2.50.
Marriage book written especially for teenagers. Based on in-depth interviews with married teens and on nationwide survey of more than three thousand teenagers' attitudes toward marriage. Extremely realistic.

_____. ***Teens Look at Marriage: Rainbows, Roles and Reality.*** 1985. 256 pp. Photos. Morning Glory Press. Hardcover, $15.95; paper, $9.95. Study Guide, $2.50.
*An in-depth coverage of the research behind **Teenage Marriage: Coping with Reality.** Attitudes of teenagers not yet married are compared with those who are married or living together. 34 bar graphs, 130 tables, 8 photos.*

_____. ***Teens Parenting: The Challenge of Babies and Toddlers.*** 1981. 308 pp. Illustrated by Pam Patterson Morford. Morning Glory Press. $9.95. Teacher's Guide, $5.95. Study Guide, $2.50.
Basic how-to-parent book based on interviews with sixty-one teenage mothers. Their comments are incorporated throughout the book. Sixth grade reading level.

_____ and Catherine Monserrat. *Adoption Awareness: A Guide for Counselors, Teachers, Nurses and Caring Others.* 1989. 288 pp. Morning Glory Press. Hardcover, $17.95; paper, $12.95.
Wonderful book for teachers, counselors, social workers, nurses, and others working with pregnant teenagers and/or older women facing untimely pregnancy. Offers an in-depth look at current adoption issues including agency, independent, and open adoption. Emphasis is on the needs of the birthparents.

_____ and Sharon Rodine. *Teen Pregnancy Challenge, Book One: Strategies for Change; Teen Pregnancy Challenge, Book Two: Programs for Kids.* 1989. 256 pp. each. Cloth, $19.95 each; two-book set, $34.95. Paper, $14.95; two-book set, $24.95. Morning Glory Press, 6595 San Haroldo Way, Buena Park, CA 90620.
A two-book set concerned with action to prevent adolescent pregnancy and to help those already pregnant or parenting avoid such problems as dropping out of school, poor pregnancy outcome, and increased risk of poverty.

McGee, Elizabeth A., with Susan Blank. *A Stitch in Time: Helping Young Mothers Complete High School.* 1989. 70 pp. Academy for Educational Development, 100 Fifth Avenue, NY, NY 10011. $15.
Guidelines for developing collaborative community strategies for addressing the needs of pregnant and parenting teenagers. Describes a three-step process for communities to follow in trying to improve the ways in which they address the educational needs of school-age mothers.

McGuire, Paula. *It Won't Happen to Me: Teenagers Talk About Pregnancy.* 1983. Delacourte, 234 pp. $14.95. Dell, 1986, $6.95.
Fifteen teenagers talk about their unplanned pregnancies, the decisions they made, and the changes in their lives.

Minor, Nancy, and Patricia Bradley. *Coping with School Age Motherhood.* Revised 1989. Rosen Group. $12.95.
Absorbing accounts of teenage parents written by the teacher and counselor in a school-age parent program in California.

Okimoto, Jean Davies, and Phyllis Jackson Stegall. *Boomerang Kids: How to Live with Adult Children Who Return Home.* 1987. 181 pp. Little, Brown and Company, Boston, MA. Paper, $3.95.

Presents guidelines for creating adult-to-adult relationship with child who returns home after having been independent. Includes an excellent chapter on three-generation living.

Parent Express Series. ANR Publications, University of California, 6701 San Pablo Avenue, Oakland, CA 94608-1239. $3/set (First Year; Toddler), payable to UC Regents.
Excellent eight-page newsletters directed to teen parents, one for each month of the first year, plus the toddler series of one every other month to age three. Reasonable reading level. Illustrated with lots of good photographs.

Peterson, Judy, Managing Editor. **Heartbeat: A Positive Parenting Magazine.** Quarterly. Women's Health and Education Foundation, 4680 Lake Underhill Road, Orlando, FL 32807. Classroom set: 25 copies, $49/year. Individual subscription, $15/year.
Beautiful full color magazine especially for teenage parents. Lots of photos.

Richards, Arlene Kramer, and Irene Willis. **What to Do If You or Someone You Know Is Under 18 and Pregnant.** 1983. 254 pp. Lothrop. Hardcover, $10.88; paper, $8.95.
A very readable discussion of possible alternatives.

Rickel, Annette U. **Teen Pregnancy and Parenting.** 1989. 225 pp. Hemisphere Publishing Company, 79 Madison Avenue, Suite 1110, New York, NY 10016. $19.95.
Comprehensive overview of teenage pregnancy and parenting in the United States. Author presents current research on the topic.

Robinson, Bryan. **Teenage Fathers.** 1988. 173 pp. Lexington Books, 125 Spring Street, Lexington, MA 02173. $25.
Excellent book on teen fatherhood. Debunks the myth of the uncaring teenage father. Combination of scholarly research brought alive with frequent vignettes from case studies of young fathers.

Roggow, Linda, and Carolyn Owens. **A Handbook for Pregnant Teenagers.** 1985. Zondervan. Paper, $4.95.
Appropriate for young women whose religious convictions make abortion an impossible choice. Alternatives of marriage, adoption, and raising the baby alone are presented.

Roles, Patricia. *Saying Goodbye to a Baby: The Birthparents' Guide to Loss and Grief in Adoption.* 1989. 92 pp. Child Welfare League of America, 440 First Street N.W., Suite 310, Washington, DC 20001-2085. $10.95.
Most of the book deals with the inevitable grieving birthparents will experience after placing their child for adoption.

Schnell, Barry T. *The Teenage Parent's Support Guide.* 1988. 135 pp. The Advocacy Center for Child Support, P.O. Box 276, Yorklyn, DE 19736. $14.95.
A guide written for teenage parents, a guide to their basic rights and obligations and to legal procedures.

Silverstein, Herma. *Teenage and Pregnant: What You Can Do.* 1988. 154 pp. Julian Messner, Simon & Schuster, Inc., Prentice Hall Building, Englewood Cliffs, NJ 07632. $5.95.
Well-written non-judgmental discussion of the issues facing pregnant teenagers.

VanDerMolen, Henrietta. *Pregnant and Alone: How You Can Help an Unwed Friend.* 1989. 160 pp. Harold Shaw Publishing, P.O. Box 567, Wheaton, IL 60189. $6.95.
Provides information and insight into helping single pregnant women. Author shares stories of thirty young women who have stayed in her home during crisis pregnancy situations. Written from a Christian perspective.

Witt, Reni L., and Jeannine Masterson Michael. *Mom, I'm Pregnant! A Personal Guide for Teenagers.* 1982. 239 pp. Scarborough House, P.O. Box 370, Chelsea, MI 48118. $6.95.
Excellent book for young people facing decisions about unplanned pregnancy.

Index

OTHER BOOKS FROM MORNING GLORY PRESS

TEENS PARENTING—Your Pregnancy and Newborn Journey
How to take care of yourself and your newborn. For pregnant teens.
Available in "regular" (RL 6), Easier Reading (RL 3), and Spanish.

TEENS PARENTING—Your Baby's First Year
TEENS PARENTING—The Challenge of Toddlers
TEENS PARENTING—Discipline from Birth to Three
Three how-to-parent books especially for teenage parents.

TEEN DADS; Rights, Responsibilities and Joys. Parenting book for
teenage fathers.

DETOUR FOR EMMY. Novel about teenage pregnancy.

SURVIVING TEEN PREGNANCY: Choices, Dreams, Decisions
For all pregnant teens—help with decisions, moving on toward goals.

BREAKING FREE FROM PARTNER ABUSE for victims of
domestic violence.

PREGNANT TOO SOON: Adoption Is an Option
Advocates choice. Young birthmothers tell their stories.

TEENAGE MARRIAGE: Coping with Reality
Gives teenagers a picture of the realities of marriage.

TEENS LOOK AT MARRIAGE: Rainbows, Roles and Reality
Describes the research behind *Teenage Marriage.*

ADOPTION AWARENESS: A Guide for Teachers, Nurses,
Counselors and Caring Others
Guide for supporting adoption alternative in crisis pregnancy.

PARENTS, PREGNANT TEENS AND ADOPTION OPTION
For all parents who feel alone as their daughter faces too-early
pregnancy and the difficult adoption/keeping decision.

DO I HAVE A DADDY? A Story About a Single-Parent Child
Picture/story book especially for children with only one parent.
Alsoavailable in Spanish (¿Yo tengo papá?)

OPEN ADOPTION: A Caring Option
A fascinating and sensitive account of the new world of adoption.

TEEN PREGNANCY CHALLENGE, Book One: Strategies for
Change; Book Two: Programs for Kids
Book One provides practical guidelines for developing adolescent
pregnancy prevention and care programs. *Book Two* focuses on
programs all along the adolescent pregnancy prevention continuum.

Please see ordering information on back of page.

MORNING GLORY PRESS

6595 San Haroldo Way, Buena Park, CA 90620
714/828-1998 — FAX 714/828-2049

Please send me the following:

		Price	Total
___*Teen Dads*	Paper, ISBN 0-930934-78-4	$9.95	_____
___	Cloth, ISBN 0-930934-77-6	15.95	_____
___*Do I Have a Daddy?*	Paper, ISBN 0-930934-44-x	5.95	_____
___*Detour for Emmy*	Paper, ISBN 0-930934-76-8	8.95	_____
___	Cloth, ISBN 0-930934-75-x	15.95	_____
Breaking Free from Partner Abuse			
___	Paper, ISBN 0-930934-74-1	$7.95	_____
Surviving Teen Pregnancy			
___	Paper, ISBN 0-930934-47-4	$9.95	_____
School-Age Parents: Three-Generation Living			
___	Paper, ISBN 0-930934-36-9	10.95	_____
Teens Parenting—Your Pregnancy and Newborn Journey			
___	Paper, ISBN 0-930934-50-4	9.95	_____
___	Cloth, ISBN 0-930934-51-2	15.95	_____
Easier Reading Edition—*Pregnancy and Newborn Journey*			
___	Paper, ISBN 0-930934-61-x	9.95	_____
Spanish—Adolescentes como padres—La jornada . . .			
___	Paper, ISBN 0-930934-69-5	9.95	_____
___**Teens Parenting—*Your Baby's First Year***			
___	Paper, ISBN 0-930934-52-0	9.95	_____
___	Cloth, ISBN 0-930934-53-9	15.95	_____
Teens Parenting—*Challenge of Toddlers*			
___	Paper, ISBN 0-930934-58-x	9.95	_____
___	Cloth, ISBN 0-930934-59-8	15.95	_____
___**Teens Parenting—*Discipline from Birth to Three***			
___	Paper, ISBN 0-930934-54-7	9.95	_____
___	Cloth, ISBN 0-930934-55-5	15.95	_____
___**Teen Pregnancy Challenge:** Bk. 1: *Strategies for Change*		14.95	_____
___	Bk. 2: *Programs for Kids*	14.95	_____
___**Pregnant Too Soon: Adoption Is an Option**		9.95	_____
___**Open Adoption: A Caring Option**		9.95	_____
___**Adoption Awareness**		12.95	_____
___**Parents, Pregnant Teens and Adoption Option**		8.95	_____
___**Teenage Marriage: Coping with Reality**		9.95	_____
___**Teens Look at Marriage**		9.95	_____

TOTAL _____

Please add postage: 10% of total—Min., $2.50   _____
California residents add 7.75% sales tax   _____

TOTAL _____

Ask about quantity discounts, Teacher, Student Guides.
Prepayment requested. School/library purchase orders accepted.
If not satisfied, return in 15 days for refund.

NAME _____

ADDRESS _____

_____